NO CREDIT REQUIRED

HOW TO BUY A HOUSE WHEN YOU DON'T QUALIFY FOR A MORTGAGE

D1016365

NO CREDIT REQUIRED

HOW TO

BUY A HOUSE

WHEN YOU DON'T QUALIFY FOR A MORTGAGE

—— REVISED EDITION ——

Ray Mungo and
Robert H. Yamaguchi

NEW AMERICAN LIBRARY

New American Library

Published by New American Library, a division of
Penguin Group (USA) Inc., 375 Hudson Street,
New York, New York 10014, USA
Penguin Group (Canada), 10 Alcorn Avenue, Toronto,
Ontario, M4V 3B2, Canada (a division of Pearson Penguin Canada Inc.)
Penguin Books Ltd., 80 Strand, London WC2R 0RL, England
Penguin Ireland, 25 St. Stephen's Green, Dublin 2,
Ireland (a division of Penguin Books Ltd.)
Penguin Group (Australia), 250 Camberwell Road, Camberwell, Victoria 3124,
Australia (a division of Pearson Australia Group Pty. Ltd.)
Penguin Books India Pvt. Ltd., 11 Community Centre, Panchsheel Park,
New Delhi - 110 017, India
Penguin Group (NZ), Cnr Airborne and Rosedale Roads, Albany,
Auckland 1310, New Zealand (a division of Pearson New Zealand Ltd.)
Penguin Books (South Africa) (Pty.) Ltd., 24 Sturdee Avenue,
Rosebank, Johannesburg 2196, South Africa

Penguin Books Ltd., Registered Offices:
80 Strand, London WC2R 0RL, England

First published by New American Library, a division of Penguin Group (USA) Inc.

First Printing (Revised Edition), November 2004

10 9 8 7 6 5 4 3 2 1

 REGISTERED TRADEMARK—MARCA REGISTRADA

LIBRARY OF CONGRESS CATALOGING-IN-PUBLICATION DATA:

Mungo, Raymond, 1946–
   No credit required : how to buy a house when you don't qualify for a mortgage / Ray Mungo and Robert H. Yamaguchi.—Rev. ed.
      p. cm.
   Includes index.
   ISBN 0-451-21310-6 (trade pbk.)
  1. House buying—United States.   2. Housing—United States—Finance.
  I. Yamaguchi, Robert H.   II. Title.
   HD1379.M77 2004
   332.7'22—dc22

                                                        2004015006

Set in Sabon
Designed by H. Saunders

Printed in the United States of America

For Nancy Mayer,
author of the popular NAL book
The Male Midlife Crisis
and real estate guru!

and
For Rita LaFontaine Mungo (1917–1996)
Ma knew best:
Get a house and don't pay rent!
—Ray Mungo

For Mitsuya Yamaguchi, MD
Thanks for the precious memories
of growing up in the house on Martel Avenue.
—Robert Yamaguchi

DISCLAIMER

All real estate purchases involve some risk, and therefore the publisher and authors cannot accept responsibility for any real estate decisions made by the reader based on the information in this book. We advise all readers to use the services of professional real estate brokers and agents and, if needed, attorneys with real estate experience.

The names and locations of home buyers described in the book have been changed to protect their privacy, but their stories are true.

The authors welcome your comments on buying real estate with no credit required, and will consider them for inclusion in possible future editions. Please address them in care of the publisher.

CONTENTS

ACKNOWLEDGMENTS

This book grew out of a passionate love affair with houses. Both of the authors have experience in buying homes with no credit required. Ray Mungo is the author of many other books, and as a self-employed writer, he found it impossible to qualify for a mortgage. But dating back to 1968 in Vermont, he has successfully purchased seven homes without credit. Robert Yamaguchi holds a doctorate in business administration and teaches college business courses in California. He has a keen interest in real estate trading and has bought and sold without credit three times since 1989.

Our aim is to show that anyone, regardless of credit history, can own a home in the United States. And we sincerely believe in that American dream, which so many have lost or given up in recent years as house prices have soared and an increasing percentage of the population can't qualify for a mortgage.

For particular help and invaluable advice, we thank the following: editor Kevin Mulroy of New American Library; editor Tracy Bernstein of New American Library; literary agents Jane Dystel and Michael Bourret; Cynthia Williams of Carmel, CA; Bob Healy and George Robbins of Morongo Valley Realty, Morongo

Valley, CA; Mortgage Bankers Association of Washington, DC; Lynne Ballew of Tokai Bank, San Diego, CA; Scott Luhrs of Century 21 Rockwell Realty, San Diego, CA; Robert J. Bruss, syndicated real estate columnist; the cooperative and helpful staff at the Federal Housing Authority and Veterans Administration, San Diego offices; Rosie Franklin, Guilford, VT; Minnie Skinner, Seattle, WA; Tim and Brenda Asire, Morongo Valley, CA; Judy Preston of Lakeshore Terrace Realty, San Diego, CA; J. Barney Malesky, manager of Palomar Realty, San Diego, CA; Bill and Nina Gerwin, Fairfax, CA; and Shirley McLaughlin of Century 21 Realty, Long Beach, CA.

Introduction

Jim and Shirley Monahan never had any credit problems while Jim was working. He made pretty good money as an insurance underwriter at an auto-body shop in San Bernardino, California, and she had bought a travel agency from her former employer in the mid-1990s. The couple loved to travel and used their credit cards liberally to take tours of France and Italy, a Caribbean cruise, and regular jaunts to a favorite resort in Maui. They figured they might as well see the world and enjoy themselves before settling down to start a family and buy a house. As home prices in southern California steadily increased, however, they became a bit nervous about getting into a place before they were priced out of the game.

Then the layoff came. After ten years on the job, Jim got exactly two weeks' notice and two months' severance pay as his employer downsized. Jim qualified for unemployment checks, but the monthly amount was paltry compared to what he was used to earning—not even enough to cover their rent. Still, he wasn't worried at first because at age forty-one and with a decent professional skill, he figured he'd find another job soon.

It wasn't soon enough. In fact, it took Jim almost a

year to get something new, and he had to settle for a lower salary, a long commute, and no health benefits.

Meanwhile, Shirley's travel agency steadily disintegrated as more and more people turned to the Internet to book their own tickets, at online prices that Shirley couldn't compete with, and airlines stopped paying commissions to travel agents. By September of 2001, Shirley had laid off her own employees and was bravely clinging to a sinking ship, alone. And on September 11 of that year, the ship sank. The terrorist attack on New York and Washington, DC, also torpedoed Joy of Discovery Travel.

In the course of these financial setbacks, the couple fell to greater dependence on their credit cards until they were using credit to buy groceries and writing credit-card checks (cash advances) to themselves to pay one account by borrowing from another.

The crash, when it came, was painful. They simply couldn't pay the bills, fell behind in their payments, tried in vain to consolidate all the debts, watched their credit rating implode, even considered filing for personal bankruptcy. Nasty bill collectors called them at all hours, stooping so low as to phone their elderly neighbors with slimy approaches like, "Would you go next door and tell Mr. and Mrs. Monahan it's urgent that they call 'Bill' at 1-800-555-5555? It's a personal matter." Embarrassed and in panic, Shirley almost regretted that she was—finally—pregnant, and both of them despaired of ever being able to buy a house and get out from under a landlord who raised their rent 10 percent every year while refusing to do repairs on their dilapidated two-bedroom house.

They cut back drastically on new purchases. No more travel, no more dining out. Still, at wildly high interest rates, their credit-card debts continued to grow. Finally they decided they needed to get a cheaper rental, to move out of the house, and to rent a smaller apartment in a less desirable neighborhood—not exactly what they wanted to bring a child into, and certainly not their original dream of home ownership.

In reading the rental ads, however, they came across a category called "Lease to Own." The ad was fetching but seemed almost too good to be true. "Lease with option to buy. $5,000 moves you in. $1,500 rent, half applies to purchase. Twelve-month lease, may be renewable. Open House Saturday, 10 AM–4 PM."

It's a time-honored strategy used by many savvy home sellers, especially when the local economy is sour or the house itself has been on the market a long time. As syndicated **real estate** columnist Robert J. Bruss has pointed out, if the seller gives the renter at least half the rent as credit toward the purchase, the renter has a terrific motivation to buy the house. But the down payment to "move you in" is not refundable if the renter never exercises the option to buy.

They drove out to the open house and fell in love with the house, if not the location. It was in a small town in the high desert, an hour's drive each way from Jim's new job. But Shirley was newly unemployed and planning to stay home and take care of the baby when it came. And the town was constructing a new elementary school right across the street from the home—a development that some home buyers would find unattractive but that fit the Monahans' needs rather perfectly.

At $190,000 the house was probably overpriced, but the sellers were determined to cash in on the inflated housing prices. They had moved out eighteen months earlier due to a job transfer to Arizona, and after a year of putting up with bad tenants who trashed the place, they were getting desperate to sell the house and be relieved of the responsibility and expense of hanging on to it.

The place needed work, all right. It needed paint inside and out, the rugs were shot, vandals had spray-painted graffiti on the garage door, and the backyard pool sat empty, black with soot and coated with desert sand. But the neighbors were middle class and pleasant, the place featured three good-sized bedrooms and a large lot, and the potential was terrific.

Best of all, the sellers were not asking for the kind of credit check required by a **mortgage** lender. They only wanted a reference from the Monahans' current landlord and proof of Jim's job (a recent pay stub).

Shirley's parents came up with the $5,000 down payment as a kind of gift to celebrate the impending birth of their first grandchild. Jim and Shirley moved in to their new home and threw themselves into repairing and remodeling it, joking all the time that if they never bought the place, the owners were getting a hell of a good deal. Imagine tenants who fix up the property at their own expense and labor while paying rent. Nonetheless, after ten months living there, the couple found they had accumulated an impressive down payment of $12,500 on the purchase—the original $5,000 plus $7,500 in rent credits. And the sellers were very happy, too. They came to trust the Monahans to pay on time and appreciated the property improvements.

As their **lease option** year was about to end, Jim and Shirley passionately wanted to complete the purchase but knew their mountain of delinquent credit-card debt would certainly make it impossible to qualify for a conventional mortgage. So Jim sat down and wrote the owners an offer he hoped they couldn't refuse. He offered to buy the house directly from the sellers and pay them a high 8½ percent **interest** on the loan. He had a friend from work print out a payment schedule that showed the owners their $190,000 house would bring them almost triple that amount over the course of a thirty-year mortgage.

The strategy worked. Since the sellers felt they could trust Jim and Shirley and were not themselves in dire need of a cash-out, they carried the mortgage. Instead of getting $1,500 a month in rent, they got $1,900 in a mortgage payment. They hired an attorney to draw up the paperwork so everything was legal and proper. One clause in the agreement stated that if Jim and Shirley were ever to sell the place, the previous owners had to be cashed out—the owner-financed mortgage was exclusive to the Monahans.

It's worth noting that the strategy would not have worked if the sellers had been more typical—that is, people who needed a cash-out at once in order to pay off their own mortgage balance. These sellers owned the house free and clear, which made it a lot easier for them to carry the mortgage. Also, they were financially well enough off not to need a lump sum payment. They were more the exception than the rule, but read on.

The tax advantages to Jim and Shirley were nothing short of stupendous. For the first time, Jim could deduct the mortgage interest and real estate taxes on his IRS return, and got a whopping refund. And owning the property seemed to improve the Monahans' credit rating overnight. Despite still owing money to Visa and MasterCard, they were deluged with home equity loan offers in their mail and e-mail. If they pay their mortgage on time for a few years, and if home prices continue to rise in California, they'll eventually be able to move up to a nicer home in a more convenient location, but they didn't need a scrap of credit to become first-time homeowners. And neither do you!

NO CREDIT, NO JOB, NO PROBLEM

No kidding! The Monahans' story is just one of many examples of how people lacking the credit to qualify for a mortgage can nonetheless buy a home. Jim and Shirley are not even close to an extreme case. Plenty of folks have bought property while having no credit at all, terrible credit with a history of bankruptcy or delinquency, no job of any kind, or a criminal record.

You can do it, too. It takes a lot of patience to find the right home, the right deal and terms. Some of these homes are available for nothing down as well, but this book is not focused on those rare properties. In truth, you can't buy a house without money—usually there will be a down payment of some kind, and there is always a monthly mortgage payment, but if you are a reasonable person who is now paying rent and somebody in your family has an income (not necessarily from a steady job), you can almost certainly buy a home *regardless of how bad or nonexistent your credit is.*

Not having good credit doesn't make you a bad person, and there's no reason to feel ashamed or reluctant to shop for a home. The national economy itself goes through periodic bouts of crisis—**foreclosures**, personal bankruptcy, and the national deficit were all at record highs in 2003. The persistent marketing of credit cards to people has put a lot of them in debt over their heads. When the unemployment rate goes up, honest people who counted on their jobs to pay their bills see their credit rating destroyed as their paychecks vanish. The entire housing industry has to adjust to everchanging conditions. If you think your **credit report** seems lousy, look at the record deficits in many state budgets.

The computer age has made it all but impossible to hide your bad credit, so you need to restrict your house hunting to deals that are explicitly "no credit required." Don't even waste your time and the real estate agent's efforts on property that requires you to **qualify**. Be honest and tell that agent up front what you need. Better yet, show him or her this book. You'll find a high percentage of agents and brokers don't know much about these deals, and some are reluctant to learn. They're caught in a mind-set of earning their commission, typically 6 percent of the sale price, and want to deal with buyers who can command a big mortgage payout from a bank or other commercial lender, many of them via the Internet. But you may be able to educate your agent about creative, unconventional ways to buy.

Of course, there are limitations and rules to follow. You can't really expect to purchase a millionaire's mansion with no credit, but you'd be surprised at what is possible. Here in California, we've seen very expensive homes advertised as "no qualifying," the magic phrase that opens the door.

Take a look at your current situation. How much do you pay in rent in a year? Whatever it is, it's money thrown in the gutter in the sense that you'll never own a stick or nail of your home no matter how many years you pay. If you've lived in the same place for a long time, you may even have already paid what the house once cost. Most parts of the nation saw a dramatic increase in home values during the 1980s, and then again in the early 2000s. Your landlords have reaped the benefits as well as all the tax advantages, while all you get is the right to occupy the premises for thirty days at a time.

Now look at the real estate prices in your neighborhood—and if they are too high, look around at other neighborhoods. Buying without credit may force you to move to a less desirable part of town, or to take on a house that needs work, or to share equity with another investor. We'll discuss all the possibilities in this book. For now, figure out what you can afford to pay every month and look for something in that range. Many people will find that they can actually own a home for no more per month than they are already paying in rent. As a general rule of thumb, the mortgage payment should be 1 percent or less of the mortgage balance— so if you owe $150,000, you'd pay $1,500 a month.

Remember, this is only a general rule. It all depends

on the interest rate on the mortgage. For a while in the early 2000s, rates were plunging, but historically they fluctuate with the market. You want an interest rate under 7 percent if possible (though a poor credit rating might force you into a much higher bracket) and a fixed rate is preferable to an adjustable, changing one.

Very few houses actively advertise themselves as "no qualifying." But many times a seller who hasn't been able to unload his or her home may be open to a no-credit suggestion. A house for sale may be available for lease option if you present the seller with an attractive offer. Many sellers can be persuaded to carry the financing themselves with the house serving as collateral, especially if the home has defects or problems that would cause a lender to refuse to issue a mortgage. (Just one example: some lenders will refuse to issue a mortgage on a **condominium** if the **condo** complex has too many renters in it.) A house that's advertised as being for rent may be for sale under the right circumstances. Use your imagination, and don't be afraid. The possibilities are endless.

Here are some of those endless possibilities. All of these will be covered in greater length in this book, and we'll illustrate them with stories of homeowners who succeeded. But just for a quick thumbnail sketch, you can buy property without credit in any combination of the following ways:

• **The assumable mortgage, both government and private.** Assuming a mortgage simply means you take over the previous owner's payments. Some federal mortgages issued by the Federal Housing Administration (**FHA**) and Department of Veterans Affairs (**VA**) are the no-qualifying variety; the original buyer had to have credit but the loan can be passed on to succeeding owners without even filling out a credit application. Unfortunately, these government deals are increasingly hard to find, since the rule is they had to originate in 1988 or earlier. Some private mortgages are assumable, too. You buy out the seller's interest and take over his payments, possibly with a second mortgage payment to the seller if you don't have enough cash to buy out his **equity** in a flat sum. We'll tell you all the rules and limits and how to look for these deals.

• **Seller financing, or "owner will carry."** This is the most typical way that people buy real estate without bank approval, and it's as popular as ever. The seller extends financing to the buyer and carries the first or sometimes a second mortgage on a private real estate contract. If the buyer fails to make the mortgage payments, the seller can take the property back and the buyer loses everything he's put into it. You can approach a seller with a proposal of owner financing in a convincing way, so that even a seller who hasn't considered it may consent because it's so much more profitable to him or her in the long run.

• **Lease with option.** You can get into a lease option purchase for a very modest amount of money and with no credit required. We offer tips and life experiences about turning a lease option into a **title** or **deed.** We advise scouring the real estate **listings** in search of vacant property that's been languishing in a slow market, cases where the seller might be relieved to have income from the house and the buyer gradually builds equity while renting.

• **The 30/70 rule.** This is a rule you won't find written down at any lending institution, but it's a common practice. A buyer who can put down 30 percent of the sale price of a house can usually get a loan for the 70 percent balance, regardless of credit. The reason is that anyone who pays 30 percent into a house is highly unlikely to walk away from the investment.

• **Adverse possession.** In most states, you can gain legal title to property without credit or even payments by open and hostile occupation of the premises. You must file adverse possession papers and take every measure to inform the rightful owner of your intentions and presence, and you must pay the real estate taxes. This is a kind of legal squatting that concludes in taking title.

• **Equity sharing.** This relatively new idea became popular in the 1980s and may be due for a renaissance in the early 2000s. One party may put up the down payment and credit, while the other invests sweat and remodeling labor; or there could be a shared living arrangement, group purchase, or **time-share** plan. The advantage to the buyer without good credit is that equity sharing provides a start in home ownership, a foot in the door.

- **Foreclosure to you.** Foreclosures of homes hit a record high during 2003, and a professional investor with ready cash can scoop up a real bargain. The foreclosure specialist then offers the house for sale at a modest down payment, with a mortgage as long as forty years at relatively high interest. The only person you have to convince of your creditworthiness is the foreclosure lender, and these deals frequently require no credit at all. You can also buy a home in or near foreclosure directly from the owner subject to an existing mortgage, which you take over. Someone else's heartache can be your homestead.

- **Quitclaim.** One of the most common and easy ways to buy without credit is to buy in joint tenancy with a relative or friend who has good credit, and have that person then quitclaim (grant) the deed to you. The original buyer's good credit remains on the line, however, which can lead to a disastrous strain on personal relationships if the payments fall behind. Quitclaiming works fine as long as trust prevails, and many a first-time buyer gets this kind of help from a parent, close friend, or ex-spouse.

- *En viager.* This is about obtaining property from the elderly or the deceased. It isn't limited to inheritance. The French have a system called *en viager* in which the property changes hands but the elderly person retains a lifetime right to occupancy. In the United States, we have life-estate grants, reverse mortgages, estate liquidation sales to settle probate, and emergency sales to pay death taxes. This doesn't have to be a grim business. After all, they couldn't take it with them, and you may be the beneficiary.

• **The unwanted, the desperate, and the ugly.** You can find property in trouble, situations where the real estate is hard to sell and therefore no credit is required to buy it. Many decent houses are virtually given away by desperate sellers who have to leave them for personal reasons, and sometimes a dilapidated fixer-upper can be a great investment. Unwanted property also includes government repossessions, vacant houses in declining urban neighborhoods, and homes abandoned in depressed rural areas.

• **Go for it!** Even if you have no credit, you can have your own piece of the rock if you want it badly enough, work for it, and keep it up. We'll tell you how. Read on.

ONE

No-Qualifying Assumable Mortgages

An assumable mortgage is a beautiful thing. Even though newer ones are less likely to be assumable, don't "assume" anything about an existing mortgage until you check it out. An assumable mortgage is simply one that you, the buyer, can take over. You make the previous owner's payments. The term of the loan, the amount owed, and the interest rate (if it's a fixed one) don't change. Owner A simply allows Owner B to take over his or her payments. Typically, you first have to pay back the seller's equity.

For example, if the seller was paying $1,008 a month on a balance of $120,000 owed on the house, you will pay the same amount and owe the same amount. If the mortgage was a thirty-year loan with six years already paid and twenty-four years to go, you'll have the same twenty-four years to go. Nothing about the mortgage changes except the person who is paying it. There is always a fee of some kind for the service of transferring the mortgage to a new owner's name, and in some cases the seller remains liable for the payment should the buyer **default**.

There is nothing particularly complicated about this mortgage—that's the beauty of it. Naturally, you should have title to the property transferred in a proper and legal fashion, handled by a reputable **escrow** company, and duly recorded in county records. The bank or lending institution will then begin mailing payment coupons or statements to you as the new owner of the house.

The escrow office is what keeps us all honest. Essentially, an escrow company holds money and legal documents and distributes them to their rightful owners at the time of closing. Of course, the escrow office charges a fee for this service, included in the **closing costs.** A very sharp seller will sometimes ask the buyer to pay half the escrow fees, but usually it's the seller's responsibility to meet the closing costs. When the escrow company closes the deal, the buyer gets the deed to the house (title), the seller gets the money coming to him, and the company records the transfer with the county recorder.

You don't absolutely need an escrow company to handle all this paperwork and monetary exchange, but we don't recommend trying a do-it-yourself job unless you're very experienced. There is just too much at stake to take a chance on errors. The escrow company is insured to cover mistakes, whereas you are not.

NO QUALIFYING

Not all assumable mortgages can be had without qualifying, however. The magic phrase to look for in the property listings in the newspaper is "no qualifying." On any given Sunday morning in a major metropolitan area paper, you might find a dozen homes labeled as such. Depending on what part of the country you live in, such listings could be scarce. They will never constitute more than a small percentage of the total number of ads in the paper. Remember that many listings with assumable mortgages don't bother to include that fact in the ad. But when you see "no qual.," you've found a seller you can work with!

You are searching for an older mortgage that the seller can pass along to anyone, with no need for the buyer himself to fill out a credit application. Such deals are not as easy to find today as they were ten or twenty years ago because the government-financed (FHA and VA) no-qualifying assumptions have to be mortgages that were originally issued before March 1, 1988 (VA) or December 14, 1989 (FHA). These older loans, if you can find one, are likely to be much lower than the current value of the property. So if you bought a $250,000 house in 2005, it might have a pre-1988 mortgage balance of only $50,000. You could assume the $50,000 mortgage, but you'd still need to come up with $200,000. Unreasonable.

There are also two privately owned mortgage lenders, Fannie Mae and Freddie Mac, which were chartered by the U.S. Congress and are overseen by the federal Department of Housing and Urban Development (HUD), so they have implicit government backing and are frequently mistaken for government programs.

Although Fannie Mae and Freddie Mac are for-profit concerns owned by shareholders, they both have programs aimed at helping people with impaired credit. Fannie Mae's My Community Mortgage program is aimed specifically for low-income people and lets you buy a house with only $500 down even if you've had credit problems in the past or would be gouged with a high interest rate by predatory banks who now issue what are called subprime mortgages at high rates to borrowers with imperfect credit histories. Fannie Mae issues mortgages to those same people at several percentage points less than the subprime lenders.

Fannie Mae is particularly proud of its record of assisting minorities and nontraditional credit risks, such as recent immigrants whose dealings are mostly in cash, and who therefore can use rent receipts and other payment documents in lieu of a credit rating.

However, neither Fannie nor Freddie is a no-credit lender dealing in assumables. They may be able to help you, but you still have to qualify by their standards. For more information, check out the Web site www. fanniemae.com.

"DUE-ON-SALE" CLAUSE

But some private mortgages continue to be assumable without qualifying—as long as they do not contain the dreaded due-on-sale clause. That clause means that any time a house is sold, the lender has the right to insist that the old mortgage be paid off. (Incidentally, lenders do not *necessarily* insist on enforcing this clause. Sometimes the interest rate on the old mortgage is higher than current rates, and the bank would prefer that you assume the existing mortgage.) If you can locate a mortgage with nothing due on sale, however, it will be infinitely easier for the seller to pass it along to you.

So how do you find an assumable mortgage? It's

easy. Ask! Ask the agent or the seller, "Does the house have an assumable mortgage with no qualifying?" Direct the agent or broker to search the listings for houses with assumable mortgages. In the age of computers, it's easily researchable. Most multiple listings will address the question: Mortgage: Assumable? Y or N (for Yes or No). Once you have located the houses with assumable mortgages in your price range and desired location, narrow the search further to those mortgages available without qualifying.

Inquire, ask around, be specific, and don't despair. You're looking for a needle in a haystack, but both authors of this book have purchased homes by assuming such mortgages, and these deals continue to exist, if not as plentifully as in the past.

Considering that absolutely no credit is required to buy certain houses, it's amusing to discover how much credit merely owning one seems to give you. Within days of closing escrow and filing a deed, you'll start receiving come-ons and pitches in the mail (and e-mail) offering home equity loans, home improvement loans, credit cards, instant cash, you-already-qualify scams, all kinds of insurance, every imaginable scheme to get the homeowner deeper into debt. These loans and lines of credit are based on the house itself as collateral, of course. You may be a former deadbeat with a sordid history of credit-card delinquency, but if you own a home you can probably borrow against it, up to a point.

BUT BE CAREFUL

The first edition of *No Credit Required* told the story of Jim and Denise Morton, a San Diego Marine and his wife, who bought a $90,000 house in San Diego in 1988 by assuming the FHA mortgage, then responded to an unsolicited offer of a $10,000 cash home-improvement loan. They fixed up the house to some extent, but Jim was called off to active duty in the first Persian Gulf war of 1990, the couple divorced, the San Diego real estate market went totally flat in the early '90s, and they wound up owing more on the place than it was worth and abandoned the property to foreclosure.

It's not difficult to imagine a similar scenario involving a soldier returning from the war in Iraq. The unsolicited offer of a home-improvement loan would likely come via e-mail ("JIM AND DENISE, YOU HAVE ALREADY QUALIFIED FOR $20,000 CASH TO IMPROVE YOUR HOME! NO CREDIT CHECK! CLICK HERE TO PROCESS!") rather than in the mail, and the young couple taking advantage of their sudden creditworthiness might spend at least part of the money on new tires for the truck, clothes for the baby, and a party for the buddies before getting around to wallpapering the bedrooms. All it would take is a soft economy and a few months of unemployment for them to be in over their heads—and headed for foreclosure. Both foreclosure and personal bankruptcy rates soared to record highs in the U.S. in the early 2000s.

THEY *BECAME* THE BANK

But other veterans have done extremely well through caution and patience. Consider the experience of Dick Paulson and his wife, Kim.

Dick and Kim met in Saigon in 1968, married in San Francisco in 1970, and wound up settling in Seaside, California, because of its proximity to Fort Ord, where Dick was stationed as a career lieutenant in the Seventh Infantry. When he retired from the military in his early forties, he became an independent contractor, while Kim took jobs cleaning houses for the rich ladies down in Carmel. It wasn't an easy life for the Paulsons, but with hard work and careful saving they raised three children, sent them all off to college, and leveraged their little VA home in Seaside all the way up to an oceanview estate in posh Pebble Beach. They needed minimal credit to get the original VA mortgage and now they sell houses to other people with no credit required.

Along the way, they learned the best racket in real estate, which is simply being the bank and collecting the interest. They bought small houses in need of repair for little down and, in most cases, no credit consideration, worked like the dickens on weekends, holidays, and evenings, and had all three kids working alongside them plastering walls, painting ceilings, and sealing roof leaks. The restored houses were rented out and then eventually sold, sometimes to the tenants, with the Paulsons acting as mortgage lender. It took twenty years, but they wound up living among the privileged rich and carrying "too much real estate," as Dick complained over a Big Mac in the McDonald's two blocks from the original family home—which he sold for $1,000 down on a personal real estate **contract** with no credit check.

The house was on busy Noche Buena Street, a couple of blocks on the "good" side of Broadway—real estate code for "safe." It had four bedrooms, two baths, a really pleasant kitchen, a big backyard with a high fence beyond which the neighbor's dogs snarled, a peek of a distant ocean view, and a retaining wall crumbling over into the next-door neighbor's yard. It wasn't in bad condition, quite well kept actually, but the negative aspects that couldn't be changed or improved were the location on a busy street, being two blocks away from "trouble," and a highly unsociable neighbor.

Beware of such *negative unchangables*, because they can make your house difficult to resell. You can always paint, wallpaper, landscape, reroof, add on, or beautify a home, but you can't change the location, the neighborhood, the local job availability and economy, the climate, or the religious/social attitudes of the people.

The only other problem with Dick's no-credit home was that it was already occupied by tenants who would probably not want to move, but also couldn't afford to buy. They were wonderful tenants who paid the $800 rent promptly every month while keeping the house spotlessly clean, and Dick figured he had to give them the courtesy of at least six months' notice to move, because it would be hard for them to find another place. That's a long time to expect a buyer to wait to get into a place, but Dick sold the house eventually, of course, and some lucky buyer got a great deal without needing to look at a banker or real estate agent. And by carrying the mortgage himself, at a steep 8 percent, Dick will turn a $120,000 property into an amazing $316,987 income if he holds the mortgage for its full thirty year term.

Dick, for his part, seems to enjoy the old neighborhood as much or more than his newfound opulence in Pebble Beach. He's still just a regular Army guy who found a hardworking, ambitious wife, and together they built a substantial life estate on the humble path of acquiring modest homes and fixing them up. By now, they've built up enough credit to walk out of any bank with millions.

If the buyers have good credit, they can simply take out a new mortgage on the place and cash out Dick and Kim. But Dick prefers to take a small down payment, act as the bank, and carry the mortgage himself in a **wraparound** deal (see the next chapter, "Owner Will Carry.")

TWO

Owner Will Carry

Suppose you can't find a house with a magical no-qualifying assumable mortgage? Or you find one, but the mortgage balance is far below the asking price, and of course you don't have the credit to qualify for a new mortgage?

Don't despair! As wonderful as an assumable mortgage is, it's *not* the most popular or conventional way that people without credit can buy a home. Without a doubt, the usual way that people buy without needing to have bank or lender approval is through seller financing. The sellers, like our friends the Paulsons in the previous chapter, act as the bank. Instead of paying a bank or mortgage company, you make out your monthly check to the previous owner(s) of the house.

With such an arrangement, you legally and absolutely own the house (and have every right to resell it) just as if you had purchased it through a bank. But the only bank you need to convince to trust you is the seller(s).

Search through the real estate classified section of your local newspaper for terms like "owner will carry," "seller financing possible," "owner MAY carry," "OWC," or "OWC 2nd." These are tip-offs that the sellers have already formed a favorable impression of carrying the financing themselves.

But don't stop there. You can also approach sellers, particularly those in danger of foreclosure, those selling "by owner," or retirees who own a house free and clear, with a convincing, written offer showing them the many advantages of carrying the financing. You can also buy property subject to existing financing, similar to assuming a mortgage, with the seller holding a second mortgage on which you make payments directly to him or her.

SAMPLE WRITTEN OFFER

(Note: this sample written offer is just a preliminary letter. If the seller agrees to your offer, you would then need to complete the more detailed private real estate contract, called a "Real Estate Purchase Contract and Receipt for Deposit," which follows in this chapter.)

March 24, 2004
To: Bob and Doris Sellers, 2345 Main St., Homesville, IL
From: Fred and Mary Buyers, 543 S. Central St., Anytown, IL
Re: Purchase Offer on Your Home
Dear Bob and Doris,

We are very impressed with all the great work you've done on your house for sale. We fell in love with your house and would like to make you an offer to purchase it for the full asking price of $135,000.

Since you own the property free and clear, we can offer you a down payment of $10,000 and monthly payments at 5.75 percent interest over a 30-year amortized mortgage with yourselves carrying the first trust deed. As you know, that interest rate is higher than many lenders now offer, and much higher than you could get on a savings account at a bank. The house could be a tidy moneymaker for you with low annual tax obligations. The figures are as follows:

Sale price: $135,000

Down payment: $10,000 at closing

Earnest money: $1,000 on signing of the Real Estate Purchase Contract and Receipt for Deposit, to be applied to the down payment

Interest rate: 5.75 percent

Term: 30 years, with no penalty for pre-payment. Sellers to be cashed out in full in the event that buyers should resell the home.

Monthly payment on mortgage balance of $125,000: $729.47, principal and interest, payable on the first of each month. Interest greatly outweighs principal in the first years of the loan.

Proceeds over the course of the loan: $262,609.20.

As you can see, your house could bring you about double the price if you carry this first mortgage. The house itself is collateral for the loan, and if the buyers should ever default on the payments, you could get the property back and keep whatever payments you received.

As evidence of income and reliability, I am enclosing copies of our last three years' IRS returns and a reference from our landlord, Bill Jones. You can also call Bill at 555-1212 and he will assure you that we have been making our rent payments of $690 a month on time for the past two years with no problems.

Please call us at your earliest convenience and we can start drawing up the paperwork. You can be one of those smart sell-

ers who carry the mortgage and reap the interest income!
Thank you for your consideration of this offer.
Sincerely,
Fred and Mary Buyers

Although not every seller is willing or able to carry
the financing, there are many excellent reasons why
they should. In the first place, the seller who carries the
financing stands to make much more money from the
sale of the house. Most mortgage payments are more
than 90 percent interest, less than 10 percent **principal**,
in the early years especially. If you're paying $1,000 a
month to the previous owner of the house, chances are
that more than $900 of it is in interest charges. You're
only gaining less than $100 on the sum you owe, the
principal balance.

In short, over a typical twenty- to thirty-year mortgage period, you will actually pay two to three times or
more the sale price of the house. If the seller carries the
loan for that long, he or she is likely to get triple the
price for the house!

That is the way mortgages are amortized, or paid
off. The system works in favor of the bank, or in these
cases, the seller who is acting as the bank. For example,
let's say you buy a house for $150,000 with owner fi-
nancing, put up a $10,500 down payment, and pay the
seller a mortgage of $139,500 over thirty years at an
interest rate of 7.25 percent. Your monthly payment,
principal and interest combined, works out to $951.64.
(You can get a complete set of mortgage **amortization**

tables from a local real estate broker, library, or book-seller, or look it up on the Internet.)

When you make the first payment of $951.64, you do not reduce the amount you owe on the house by very much. In fact, only a dollar or so goes against the principal amount owed, whereas $950 of the $951 is interest paid. The $139,500 owed is down to $139,499.

With every month that passes, the proportion of interest goes down and principal goes up. Halfway through the thirty years, your $951 is evenly divided, half to interest and half to principal.

If you make this same payment every month for the full thirty years, you will have paid $342,590 on that $139,500 mortgage, or about $203,000 in interest. The seller winds up collecting $353,090, about two and a half times the price of the house, over time.

The property itself is the security for the loan, so if you fail to make your payments, the seller always has the option to foreclose and take the house back, in which case you'd lose every dime you put into it. But the average seller doesn't want to think about such a possibility any more than you, the buyer, would. He doesn't want the house back! The seller just wants to find buyers who are definitely and positively going to come up with the payment, so he or she can be free of worry. And the house itself provides a kind of consoling security; typically, it's where the seller himself has lived and is regarded as a well known and safe investment. There's always a risk that a buyer will default on the payments, or neglect or even trash the property, but that risk is diminished proportionately to the amount of money the buyer has put into it. If you've invested thousands of your hard-earned dollars into a house, you're not likely to let it go to rot or lose it to foreclosure except under dire circumstances. (Foreclosure, of course, can happen. See the chapter on "Foreclosure to You" for tips on how you can benefit from others' misfortunes.)

What kind of people will agree to finance the sale of their house? You'd be surprised. They don't have to be rich, but they have to be comfortable enough that they don't need to cash out of their house on selling it. Some owners simply must cash out because they need the money to purchase another home or for some other urgent reason. But a lot of sellers already have another place to move, and for tax reasons in addition to the great income, they prefer to carry the mortgage.

• Older people about to retire or move into assisted living, a convenient apartment, or an adult child's home, are excellent candidates for seller financing. If the children have grown and moved out, and/or a spouse has died, an elderly seller may want to be rid of the work, expense, and stress of maintaining a big home. For such a person, seller financing provides a stable monthly check, a comfortable retirement income instead of scraping by on Social Security or a limited pension. If he or she dies before the mortgage is paid off, you continue making the payments to the heirs or the estate. It's a way that someone can provide an inheritance and stable income to a beloved grandchild or alma mater.

• Sellers trapped in a slow (or dead) real estate market may consider financing the sale themselves, because it makes a home much easier to sell. With seller financing, you can close escrow in a matter of days, not the weeks or months required by mortgage lenders. There are no lengthy bank forms and excruciatingly complicated credit checks to fill out; documentation can be clean and simple.

• If you find a house that's been on the market for at least six months without a sale, you're more likely to find a seller who'll at least consider an offer to finance the deal. If you can come up with a decent down payment (sometimes not even that), the seller may prefer to carry the financing and get a monthly check rather than have the house sit there, unsold, producing nothing but heartache.

• Property in bad condition is a prime candidate for an owner-will-carry sale. Banks and lending institutions have certain standards for the house as well as the purchaser, and often if the house has a particular defect (like a cracked slab **foundation**, or no foundation at all, a small lot that prohibits additions, a zoning problem, an illegal mother-in-law apartment that must be torn down, or a condominium in a complex that has too many renters and not enough owner-occupants), no bank will issue a mortgage on it—no matter how good the buyer's credit may be. In such cases—and there are many— the seller has no choice but to carry the loan unless he or she can find a buyer willing to pay all cash up front or unless he/she's willing to let you take over the payments (buying subject to the existing financing) while continuing to be legally responsible for the debt.

BUYER BEWARE!

If you get into an owner-financed deal on a house that no bank will touch, you're going to have the same problem yourself when you or your heirs try to sell the house someday—unless you can fix the underlying problem. (And let's face it, sooner or later the house will probably be sold again. Very few Americans keep a house from generation to generation. We're a mobile culture.)

Therefore, consider these points:

1. Make sure whatever defect the house has is something you can comfortably live with, or better yet, something you can fix. On the West Coast and in the Sunbelt states, some houses lack foundations, but the weather is mild, so you don't really need a basement. The bank may disapprove, but you may not even care. You can always jack up a house and put a foundation under it, but that's complicated and costly. Other defects are much simpler and cheaper to fix.

2. If you buy a house that's got something wrong with it that prohibits a bank mortgage, you don't want a due-on-sale clause in your mortgage. That kind of clause allows the seller to demand payment in full in the event you resell the house, and that'll be almost impossible if the place can't qualify for a conventional loan. You want the right to sell the house to still another buyer and finance it yourself. Some houses are carried from owner to owner like that through three or even four mortgages.

3. Sellers who have already moved (because of a job transfer or other personal reasons) are good candidates to carry the financing. If the house is empty and the owner is still paying his own mortgage plus taxes and insurance, as well as the expenses on the new home, he or she may be financially distressed and happy to have someone else—anyone else— paying for the old property.

4. Owners who have already paid off their mortgages are in great shape to finance your purchase. They don't even have to make a payment themselves and can pocket every cent of your payment. But even those who are still paying off their own mortgages can sometimes finance yours in a wraparound mortgage. A wraparound is one in which the buyer pays the seller a monthly mortgage payment, while the seller continues to pay an existing earlier mortgage. Legally, it's sometimes called an "overriding or all-inclusive trust deed." If the seller's own mortgage has a due-on-sale clause, the bank has the right to be cashed out when the house is sold. Therefore, the seller could probably not finance a wraparound. And government-backed mortgages such as FHA and VA loans cannot by law be "subjugated" to an overriding wrap. Nonetheless, plenty of sellers can do a wraparound (they are also popular in commercial property transactions), and the wraparound is a great opportunity for the buyer without credit.

5. Sometimes a seller who is reluctant to carry a mortgage may be willing to do so if you set a reasonable time limitation followed by a **balloon payment.** In other words, the seller agrees to finance you for five years, for example, at the end of which time you agree to find new financing and cash the seller out for whatever amount is still owed on the house. The assumption here—no guarantee—is that after five years, the property will be worth far more than when you bought it, and you'll be able to find new financing more easily. A big balloon payment is always a risk, but it's a very common practice in private real estate contracts, and it usually works fine. (But you may lose sleep as that balloon approaches. . . .) You can also turn around and sell the property just before the balloon falls due! Author Ray Mungo did precisely that in Seattle, three times, and walked away with a profit every time.

6. Location is everything, according to the old real estate adage. A house in a great location, where most people would love to live, is not as likely to be available without credit or through seller financing. (Although there are exceptions to this and every rule in real estate.) Generally, if the location of the house is somewhat less than perfect, you've got a better chance. But please don't go out and buy a house sitting next door to the county dump because it's cheap and offers seller financing. Choose a location with enough natural appeal that you'll be able to sell the house to someone else someday.

7. Remember that houses for *rent* and houses that don't specifically offer owner financing may still be available without credit through owner-will-carry techniques. It's simply up to you to convince the landlord/owner to sell it to you on that basis. Countless people have purchased their first home from the landlord after renting it for years. Here's where it pays to get creative. Make your landlord an offer he can't refuse—one in which you'll put up a good-sized down payment and increase the amount of money you send him every month if he'll sell you the same place you're already renting.

8. If you don't feel you can be creative enough to pull it off, you can always seek out a "buyer's agent," a real estate agent who will make the offer for you. Seller financing deals often don't require an agent, however. In some cases, the seller is determined to avoid paying the agent's commission. Any seller willing to carry the mortgage is probably sophisticated enough to write up the deal without needing an agent's services and without having to pay that commission. If a sales agent brings you to the home and writes up the purchase, the seller will have to pay that person's commission even if he carries the financing, so some sellers will flatly refuse to deal with agents. If you see the phrase "principals only" in an ad, it means just that.

We are not opposed to agents. To the contrary, we believe that in *most* cases it is preferable to use one—yes, even with owner financing. Many people just don't know how to construct a legal, binding agreement, and the intricacies of the real estate contract may be too daunting. A good, reputable agent also acts as a third-party buffer between seller and buyer, and can negotiate the terms back and forth with less emotional involvement than the principal players. We recommend your looking for an experienced agent who's handled many no-credit deals in the past. The choice of an agent is important because a small percentage of highly successful ones handle the overwhelming majority of property transfers in most markets. When shopping for an agent, ask for references to homeowners who have worked with that person in the past. Look for someone with a track record.

In addition to agents and brokers, some attorneys also specialize in real estate law, and you can hire such a lawyer to represent you in the transaction, draw up paperwork, and generally make certain that everything is proper and in good order. Just as with an agent, look for a lawyer who has extensive experience in home-purchase contracts. (See the real estate contract form at the end of this chapter. You can use this form word for word for your purchase or get a similar document from any well-stocked stationery store or online.)

HOW TO TALK THE SELLER INTO BEING THE BANK

If the house is being advertised with owner-will-carry terms, you just have to convince the seller that you're capable of meeting his or her price and terms. But if you have to convince the seller to carry the financing, you will need to be more creative and persuasive. Here's some good and time-tested advice:

• **Make your offer in writing.** Oral or spoken agreements have no worth at all in real estate transactions. Only a formal offer in writing can initiate a sale, and that written offer is what the seller is waiting to see. Of course, you can talk about the house and your offer all you want, but unless you get it on paper, it's not an offer. Use the standard purchase offer form you can get at a stationer's or online, the kind that makes several carbon copies.

• **Show the seller how much he or she is going to profit from carrying the financing.** A lot of people don't realize how much more they could get for their home by carrying the mortgage. The Smiths are selling their $125,000 home and still owe $75,000 on it, so they figure they're going to get about $50,000 out of the sale. If, instead, you gave them $10,000 down and pay them about $900 a month at 8 percent interest, it's possible they could wind up receiving $325,000 for their $125,000 property. If you can demonstrate to a seller exactly how much money he'll get by being the bank, he may go for it.

Use standard mortgage amortization interest tables, which you can get from your bank, savings and loan, local real estate office, or over the Internet.

• **Convince the seller that you have the means to make the payments on time, without fail.** This gets tricky, of course, since you have inadequate credit, or perhaps none at all. But if you can't make the payments on time, you shouldn't be buying the house. If there's anyone in your household who has a steady job, inform the seller of this stable employment and prove to him what the salary is by showing pay stubs or tax returns. Offer the employer's name and phone number as a reference.

• If you're self-employed, it might help to present the seller with copies of your IRS 1040 tax returns from the last three years. (Unless of course they prove beyond a doubt that you're losing money in your business.)

• If you're now paying rent and are not behind in rent payments, by all means give the seller your landlord's name and phone number as a reference. This can be the ultimate convincing strategy. If you're trying to take on a $1,000 mortgage payment and you've been paying $800 rent in a timely fashion every month, the seller has every reason to believe you can swing it. On the other hand, if your rent is only $600 and you're trying to move up to a $1,200 mortgage obligation, you may have to do a bit more convincing.

• Do you have assets other than income or job, something that could literally be cashed out if the need arose? Don't hesitate to give the seller a list of these things and document their existence with photocopies of ownership documents (like the pink slip on a car or evidence of a modest stock portfolio). A lot of folks without good credit nonetheless own a fine automobile, a valuable collection of baseball cards or some other collectible items, family heirlooms, jewelry, electronic equipment, you name it. Make a complete inventory.

• **Offer some kind of down payment, no matter how modest.** You can still buy property for nothing down in some circumstances, but the average seller will be insulted by such an offer. The owner has probably put a great deal of money and work into the house over a long period, and the idea of getting nothing up front for selling it will be painful. It's an emotional as well as financial transaction when you're dealing directly with the seller. Banks sometimes insist on a down payment as high as 20 percent of the sale price, and it would be great if you could come up with 10 percent down in a seller-financed deal, but these guidelines are general and completely open to negotiation. If you're out of work, struggling with debts, or otherwise having credit difficulties, even 5 percent down may be too much. But offer something—not nothing—down. Dick Paulson in the previous chapter was willing to take $1,000 down on a house worth more than $120,000. Why? "Because the thousand bucks tells me they're serious," he said. "If you can get in there with nothing down, it's just like paying rent. Then if they stop making payments it could take me months to evict them and I've got nothing for my trouble, and they could even trash the house." A mere thousand made that much difference to him.

• **Find a house advertised for rent and offer the landlord more than the rent if he'll sell it with owner financing.** Throw in a down payment, too. If the asking price for the rent is $990 a month, go to the landlord and say, "I'll give you $1,200 a month for that house and $X,000 down if you'll sell it to me on a private real estate contract with owner financing." The bigger the down payment, the better, from the landlord's point of view. Right away, he's getting extra thousands up front and getting a much higher monthly payment, with the property itself as security for the loan. If the landlord happens to be financially strapped or even just a little greedy, he or she may accept your offer. In any case, you have nothing to lose by trying.

THE FINE ART OF NEGOTIATION

All of the above-suggested tactics are part of the art of negotiation, which is a human-relations tool at which some people are more successful than others. You may be the kind of person who feels nervous about approaching a landlord or seller with a proposal, or embarrassed by talking to real estate agents about your need for a no-credit deal. You may worry that you don't have the skill to write a document that's convincing, legal, and safe. There's no guaranteed script you can simply follow, but consider these suggestions:

- **Know yourself.** Who's going to know you better? Ask yourself if you are capable of this kind of negotiation; and if you find that you're not, get some help. Even if you are the sole buyer, there's no reason why a family member, a friend, or a competent real estate agent or attorney can't negotiate the deal on your behalf. It could be well worth the expense of having a professional draw up the papers or sweet-talk the seller, if that's what it takes to get you into a house without credit.

- **Know the other person.** Of course you probably won't know the seller or agent in a personal sense, but if you can put yourself in the other person's shoes, if you can empathize with what they must be feeling and what they want, that skill can take you a long way, all through the transaction. Ask yourself, if I were the seller, how would I feel? How much would I want to get out of it? What would make me feel more secure?

Selling a house is a hugely emotional event for most people, maybe even more so than buying one. The seller may have spent decades in his or her home, raising a family or having pets, being married or sharing with a loved one, experiencing all the ups and downs life offers. As corny as it sounds, many a seller has been swayed by personal feelings about the buyer. Will the buyer keep up his beloved backyard trees? Does the buyer really appreciate the hand-made trellis, the specialty wallpaper, the custom-decorated breakfast nook? It doesn't hurt a bit to flatter the seller's sense of aesthetics. It helps a lot to have things in common—maybe you're both dog lovers, perhaps you have the same number of children . . . anything that can personalize your relationship is a plus.

• **Don't say too much.** Don't go overboard on this suggestion to the point of revealing everything about yourself, including your fondness for broccoli and your shoe size. Keep closely focused on appealing to the seller's needs, making the deal as attractive as possible. A lot of unnecessary personal information just acts as a distraction. You want to get personal only in areas where you can make yourself seem like the perfect buyer for the house, someone who respects all the love and sweat the seller has put into his or her home.

• **Don't say too little.** Don't neglect to add every detail that can strengthen your case. It might help you to sit down and discuss the prospective house purchase with a friend or trusted coworker, family, a teacher, a counselor, your religious leader, anyone you consider smart who might come up with new ideas that you hadn't thought about. You want to make the best case you can, and that means including every detail that helps portray you as a responsible person who will absolutely take care of the property and meet your financial obligations on it, no matter what, despite your history of poor or no credit.

• **Be positive.** Keep the tone of your negotiation upbeat and optimistic. If you have your doubts about some aspects of the house, and surely you will, it's best not to voice them in a critical or badgering way, especially with the seller. There are gentle ways to express concerns, rather than bludgeoning the issue. One of the delicate skills of negotiation is the art of delivering negative information in a soft, positive fashion. So be vague, not aggressive: "I wonder, if . . . maybe . . . that roof might need replacement sometime in the future?"

• **Do your homework.** Find out everything you can about real estate values, neighborhood concerns, taxes, trends in employment, and the quality of local schools surrounding the house you want to buy. The more you know, the more you will impress the seller with your sincerity, and you'll negotiate better because you know what you're talking about. (Doing this kind of detective work might also protect you from buying something you don't really want.)

• **Meet the neighbors.** Neighbors frequently talk to each other, and this simple tactic is usually overlooked, but if you want to know the seller's mind-set better, and also learn more about the house and the neighborhood, there's no better approach than simply ringing the doorbells of the nearest neighbors. If you make a good impression, there's a chance the neighbor might speak well of you to the seller, and create a positive influence. In any case, if you're seriously negotiating to buy the house, you're better off knowing who's living next door.

• **Be confident. Subscribe to the American Dream.** If you feel your confidence wavering, if you fear you just can't negotiate a deal, stop and remember that you are not the first or only person in need of a home but lacking credit. Millions of Americans are in the same position and yet manage to succeed in achieving home ownership. Believe in yourself and hold your head high.

SOME TYPICAL MORTGAGE TABLES

Complete mortgage tables could literally take up hundreds of pages here, because they vary widely, based on three factors:

• The interest rate

• The length or term of the loan

• The amount of the principal, or the amount owed

In the 1980s, we saw inflated interest rates in the high teens; 14 to 17 percent was not uncommon. A decade later, in the practical 1990s, the opposite trend took place. Fixed rates descended to 8 percent and adjustable rates lower than that. Now in the mid-2000s, in what's been called a soft depression, mortgage interest rates have plunged to as low as 4 percent and are often touted online via Internet, and sometimes with no human interaction required. There's simply no way to guarantee here what interest rates are going to do in the future, because they react to the health of the economy in general. That's another good reason to stay away from the adjustable rates, which can change so drastically as to make it impossible for you to keep up your payments.

For the sake of example, then, let's look at a couple of mortgage amortization tables ranging between 5 and 8 percent for amounts ranging from $50,000 to $200,000, over a period of ten to thirty years. Note how much difference even a fraction of a percentage point can make.

MONTHLY MORTGAGE PAYMENT AT 5% INTEREST

TERM	10 YEARS	20 YEARS	30 YEARS
AMOUNT of mortgage:			
$ 50,000	530.33	329.98	268.41
65,000	689.43	428.97	348.93
95,000	1,007.62	626.96	509.98
125,000	1,325.82	824.94	671.03
155,000	1,644.02	1,022.93	832.07
200,000	2,121.31	1,319.91	1,073.64

MONTHLY MORTGAGE PAYMENT
AT 5¾% INTEREST

TERM	10 YEARS	20 YEARS	30 YEARS
AMOUNT of mortgage:			
$ 50,000	548.85	351.04	291.79
65,000	713.50	456.35	379.32
95,000	1,042.81	666.98	554.39
125,000	1,372.12	877.60	729.47
155,000	1,701.42	1,088.23	904.54
200,000	2,195.38	1,404.17	1,167.15

MONTHLY MORTGAGE PAYMENT
AT 6⅛% INTEREST

TERM	10 YEARS	20 YEARS	30 YEARS
AMOUNT of mortgage:			
$ 50,000	558.25	361.83	303.81
65,000	725.72	470.38	394.95
95,000	1,060.67	687.48	577.23
125,000	1,395.62	904.58	759.51
155,000	1,730.56	1,121.67	941.80
200,000	2,232.99	1,447.32	1,215.22

MONTHLY MORTGAGE PAYMENT
AT 6¾% INTEREST

TERM	10 YEARS	20 YEARS	30 YEARS
AMOUNT of mortgage:			
$ 50,000	574.12	380.18	324.30
65,000	746.36	494.24	421.59
95,000	1,090.83	722.35	616.17
125,000	1,435.30	950.46	810.75
155,000	1,779.37	1,178.56	1,005.33
200,000	2,296.48	1,520.73	1,297.20

MONTHLY MORTGAGE PAYMENT
AT 7¼% INTEREST

TERM	10 YEARS	20 YEARS	30 YEARS
AMOUNT of mortgage:			
$ 50,000	587.01	395.19	341.09
65,000	763.11	513.74	443.41
95,000	1,115.31	750.86	648.07
125,000	1,467.51	987.97	852.72
155,000	1,819.72	1,225.08	1,057.37
200,000	2,348.02	1,580.75	1,364.35

MONTHLY MORTGAGE PAYMENT AT 8% INTEREST

TERM	10 YEARS	20 YEARS	30 YEARS
AMOUNT of mortgage:			
$ 50,000	606.04	418.22	366.88
65,000	788.63	543.69	476.95
95,000	1,152.61	794.62	697.08
125,000	1,516.59	1,045.55	917.21
155,000	1,880.58	1,296.48	1,137.34
200,000	2,426.55	1,672.88	1,467.53

(Note: Mortgage payment is principal and interest combined. Taxes and insurance are extra.)

Analyzing these figures, you'll find that if you are carrying a mortgage balance of $200,000, your monthly payment could be anywhere between $1,073.64 and $2,426.55, which is a huge difference, depending on the interest rate and how long the mortgage term is. (Realistically, not many people opt for the short ten year mortgage. And these days, forty year terms are not unknown.) And remember, that's only between 5 and 8 percent. If the interest were only 3 or 4 percent or as high as 11 or 12 percent, the difference would be even more staggering.

Consider this, too: at 5 percent amortized over ten years, you would pay a total of *$254,557.20* on a $200,000 mortgage. On the same mortgage amount, except at 8 percent and amortized over thirty years, you would pay a total of *$528,310.80*, more than twice as much.

If you can show the seller figures like this—solid indications of how much profit there is in extending seller financing—you just might convince someone to be your bank.

A final note: although standard tables are available at your bank, real estate office, library, or bookstore, any banker or real estate agent can tell you in an instant exactly what your mortgage payment would be just by plugging into the computer the amount, term, and interest rate. You can easily do the same on a home computer.

THE PRIVATE REAL ESTATE CONTRACT

A private real estate contract between buyer and seller is just like a bank-mortgaged purchase agreement in that it is a legal document stating *all* the particulars of the sale. You may want to have an attorney with real estate experience check the document before you sign, and you'll almost certainly want to use an escrow company. Just as in most deals, you'll be expected to produce a check for **earnest money,** usually a small amount used to open an escrow account. How small is small? That depends on the cost of the house, but it's entirely negotiable. In some cases, $500 to $1,000 will be enough. The only danger is that if you change your mind and back out of the deal, the earnest money may not be refundable. The seller may get to keep it in exchange for releasing the buyer from the sale. Always make your earnest money check out to the real estate agency or the escrow company, not directly to the sellers.

The contract contains the full names of all sellers and buyers, a legal description of the property (available from your county recorder's office—the street address of the house is usually not sufficient to constitute a legal description), the price of the property and all the terms (including the amount of down payment, the amount of monthly payment, the interest rate of the loan, the number of years the mortgage is to run, the balloon payment if any, the agent's commission if any), a date of purchase and projected date of closing.

Many other details can be added to the contract. If the house has **fixtures** or personal property that are included in the sale, they should be mentioned specifically. You don't want an argument later when you discover the sellers have removed the blinds, curtains, chandelier, or the refrigerator you admired. It's better to spell everything out in the most specific terms: include a list of all the things that will remain with the property. In some states, the sellers are also required to sign a list of disclosures, essentially guaranteeing that everything in the house is in working order, or else specifically naming problems or needed repairs. It is illegal for someone to hide known defects in the house they sell you, but beware—to get legal recourse later, you'd have to prove that the seller knew of the defect and deliberately lied about it. Be sure to get the disclosures in writing at the outset.

If the seller insists on a clause stating the house is being sold **as is**, be especially wary, as it almost always means there's some problem(s) that the seller doesn't want to be held responsible for in the future.

The seller must promise in writing to deliver a valid, legal, and clear title to the property. This assures you that there isn't some other person or institution with a claim to the deed. In most cases, it's wise to take out a **title insurance** policy, which for a modest fee will cover you in case your title is clouded by previous claimants.

Insurance and taxes figure into this private contract, too. Always insist that the seller maintain insurance on the house at least equal to the sale price up to the day of closing, and always make arrangements for your new insurance policy to begin at the same time. The house should never be left uninsured for a moment. What if it burns down while you're at the escrow office signing papers?

Of course the contract must be dated and properly signed by both sellers and buyers. Sometimes the escrow company or agent will need your signatures verified by a notary, especially if you can't be there in person for the closing ceremonies. We recommend that you do attend in person, just for the thrill of being handed the deed to the ranch. But never try to make last-minute changes to the deal just as you're about to close; you could create problems that kill the sale or postpone it indefinitely. Get your private real estate contract in good order and you shouldn't need to amend anything later.

(You can copy this contract word for word, typing it out on white paper, or get a standard form at a stationery store. In any case, read it to familiarize yourself with the contract and its terms.)

Real Estate Purchase Contract and Receipt for Deposit
Name of city and state, Date_____ , 20_____

Received from _____ (hereinafter called "Buyer") the sum of
_____ dollars ($_____) evidenced by cash ( ),
cashier's check ( ), personal check ( ), or _____ ( ),
payable to _____, to be held uncashed until acceptance of
this offer, as deposit on the account of the total purchase price of
_____ dollars ($_____) for the purchase of that certain
real property and all improvements located thereon situated in
_____County, state of _____, and described as follows:
_____
_____

(legal description of the property)

1. Buyer will deposit in escrow with (*name of escrow
holder*) the total purchase price as follows:
    A. The above deposit shall be delivered by Broker ( )
    Seller ( ) to the escrow holder promptly upon Seller's
    acceptance hereof for the accounting of the Buyer.
    B. The total cash down payment to be deposited with es-
    crow, including the above amount, is _____ dollars
    ($_____).
    C. Seller's Purchase Money Carryback. The balance of
    the purchase price is to be evidenced by a Note secured
    by a Trust Deed on the property in the amount of
    _____ dollars ($_____), executed by the Buyer in
    favor of the Seller, including interest at _____ percent
    (%) per annum, to accrue from close of escrow. Principal
    and interest payable monthly in installments of _____
    dollars ($_____) or more, beginning on the first day
    of each month after the close of escrow. A late charge of

_____ dollars ($_____) shall be due on any payment tendered more than ten (10) days late. This is an all-inclusive Note secured by a Deed of Trust for a total purchase price of _____ dollars ($_____).

2. Upon mutual execution of this contract, the parties shall execute escrow instructions to the escrow holder in accordance with the terms and provisions hereof, which shall constitute joint instructions to the escrow holder. The parties shall execute additional instructions requested by the escrow holder not inconsistent with the provisions hereof. Said escrow shall provide for a closing on or before (*date*).

3. As soon as reasonably possible after opening of escrow, Seller shall provide the Buyer a Preliminary Title Report on the subject property, together with full copies of all exceptions set forth therein, including but not limited to covenants, conditions, restrictions, reservations, easements, rights and rights of way, liens and other matters of record. Buyer shall have _____ ( ) days after receipt of said Preliminary Title Report within which to notify the Seller and the escrow holder, in writing, of Buyer's disapproval of any exceptions shown in said Title Report. Seller shall have until the date of closing of escrow to attempt to eliminate any disapproved exceptions from the policy of Title Insurance to be issued in favor of Buyer and, if not eliminated, then the escrow shall be canceled unless Buyer elects to waive his prior disapproval. Failure of Buyer to disapprove any exceptions within the aforementioned time limit shall constitute approval of said Preliminary Title Report. The policy of Title Insurance shall be issued by (*name of title insurance company*) with a liability limited to the total purchase price and shall be paid for by Seller.

4. Seller shall furnish a structural pest control report showing accessible areas of buildings upon the property to be free of infestation caused by wood-destroying insects, fungi, or dry rot. Seller shall pay for any corrective work required.

5. Title shall vest as follows: *name of title holder(s)*

6. Buyer and Seller agree that fixtures and fittings attached to the property, including but not limited to window shades, curtains, blinds, built-in and attached appliances, light fixtures, plumbing fixtures, carpeting, air conditioners, trees, shrubs, mailbox and other similar items, if applicable, are included, but no personal property except as specified below:

7. If Buyer fails to complete said purchase as herein provided by reason of any default of Buyer, Seller shall be released from any obligation to sell the property to Buyer and may proceed against Buyer upon any claim or remedy in law. By placing their initials here, however, Buyer (   ) and Seller (   ) agree that Seller shall retain the deposit as his liquidated damages.

8. Possession shall be delivered to Buyer on close of escrow.

9. Real property taxes and premiums on insurance on the forementioned property shall be prorated between Seller and Buyer as of the date of closing of escrow. Buyer and Seller agree to each pay one half (½) of escrow fees.

10. If the property is destroyed or materially damaged between the date of this contract and the date of closing of escrow, Buyer shall have the option to declare in writing that this contract is null and void, and under such circumstances Seller shall waive any right to retain Buyer's deposit.

11. This constitutes a legal and binding offer to purchase the above described property. Unless acceptance is signed by Seller and delivered to Buyer in person or by mail to the address below, within _____ days from the date hereof, this offer shall be revoked and the deposit returned to Buyer. Buyer acknowledges receipt of a copy hereof.

SIGNED:

Broker:_____   Buyer:_____

Address:_____   Address:_____

_____   _____

Phone:_____   Phone:_____

ACCEPTANCE

The undersigned Seller accepts and agrees to sell the above described property on the above terms and conditions. Seller has employed *(name of broker)* and agrees to pay a commission for services rendered in the amount of _____ dollars ($_____) upon closing of escrow and recording of deed or other evidence of title, OR if the completion of the sale is prevented by default of Seller, upon Seller's default. The undersigned Seller acknowledges receipt of a copy of this contract and authorizes Broker to deliver a signed copy to Buyer.

Seller:_____   Broker:_____

Date:_____   Date:_____

Address:_____   Address:_____

_____   _____

Phone:_____   Phone:_____

NOTES ON THIS REAL ESTATE CONTRACT

This is a highly simplified version of the contract, based on a number of actual ones that the authors have observed in past transactions. Every real estate contract should include these basic clauses, but some will add many more.

People sometimes think there is a formal, set, correct way to do this, and in fact you should have the legal protection of at least these three elements: a solid title insurance policy, proper vesting of title, the securing of a bonded escrow holder.

You can buy a title insurance policy from any reputable title insurance company. In most towns, an escrow company or real estate broker will be glad to recommend a local title insurance company. (They usually work together.) Your best safety is in the longevity and reputation of that company. Basically, title insurance companies take the risk of a bad or flawed title away from you and onto their own shoulders. Typically, they research ownership of the house for as many years in the past as they can find records. Those records of past transfers of title can make for some very entertaining reading on winter nights, while you are enjoying the warmth of your new home!

Vesting of title refers to the name or names in which the deed is to be recorded. To vest means simply to bestow upon. The former owner vests the title on you, the new owner. Be sure that title is vested to your formal, proper name(s). Don't have title vested to Don Jones if your name is Donald Anthony Jones III. As far-fetched as it might sound, there could be some other Don Jones somewhere who could contest your title.

The real estate broker's commission is also completely open to negotiation. If an agent tells you the standard commission is 6 percent or whatever, don't believe it. There is no such thing as a standard commission, but there is a typical rate in any given area. Let your agent make an honest living. But especially with owner financing, you can sweeten the deal for the seller by operating without an agent or lowering the commission rate offered.

Taxes are an important issue, of course. In many cases, the mortgage payment will include both the taxes and insurance in monthly installments, so make only one payment, and you're covered. But in other instances, you'll have to pay your local or state government a real estate tax that is levied once or twice a year. If you're buying a house, be sure to find out how much the taxes are and how they are paid.

There is no standard real estate tax rate; it varies from place to place. The state of New Hampshire, which has no sales or income tax, compensates somewhat with relatively high property taxes. In California, taxes were actually rolled back in the 1980s due to a voters' initiative.

The tax you pay on your home will be determined by the local tax rate and the government's assessed value of your property. These **assessments** are frequently lower than the fair **market value**, especially if one owner has held the property for a long time.

Always make sure that your tax is paid, because the government can eventually take the property away from you and sell it at auction to pay off back taxes.

THREE

Owners Who Carried, and How It All Worked Out

Author Ray Mungo was one of a group of good friends who got together in 1968 and bought a one hundred-acre farm in Vermont from an elderly widow who had spent most of her life on the property, saw her children grow and move out and her husband die there. She just wanted a reliable monthly income to help finance her retirement nest in an "all-electric apartment" in the nearby town of Brattleboro. The farm had only wood heat and a very limited **septic tank** (requiring use of an outhouse), was located on a steep dirt road, was often snowed in during winter, and generally lacked the comforts and proximity to services that most elderly people need.

The group just wanted a retreat from urban stress in New York and Washington, a place in the country where artists and writers could gather to work in peace and recharge their batteries.

Rosie Franklin, the widow, was nobody's fool. She realized that if she sold the property for cash, she'd have an enormous tax liability and lose a big part of her money. She also knew that by carrying the mortgage, she would eventually get twice the price of the house and acreage. But since she was in her early seventies and couldn't know for certain that she'd live another twenty years, she insisted on a ten-year mortgage, at 10 percent interest. The group bought the place for $25,000 with a $5,000 down payment and a mortgage payment of $227.10 a month. That was real money in 1968. Rosie added a provision that although the group was buying her farm and would own it, she retained the lifetime right to pick peaches from the orchard once a week during harvest time. This was a delightful touch, and the group didn't mind sharing the peaches with her in the least.

On the first day of every month, someone went into town and gave Rosie her $227.10—sometimes in cash, for which she gave them a handwritten receipt, and then they checked off another payment on the mortgage balance printout, which was posted on the kitchen wall. There were occasions when they couldn't come up with the entire $227.10 at once, so they paid Rosie whatever amount they had scraped up and finished the payment later in the month. They never actually got a full month behind in the payments, and Rosie was always sympathetic and understanding when they were hard up, but she literally needed that mortgage payment to pay her own rent, groceries, and doctor bills, and the group felt responsible. She also held the farm itself as collateral for the loan, so if they'd failed to pay she could have exercised her right to take the property back.

Ten years later, the note was paid and now, more than thirty years later, the property is very valuable and still in the hands of the group—incorporated as a nonprofit artist cooperative. They were lucky that they bought property in Vermont while the state was economically depressed and before the great surge of back-to-the-land urban refugees began arriving in the '70s. Skiers started coming in great numbers, classical music festivals sprang up, and it became chic for New Yorkers and Bostonians to own a chalet in Vermont.

When the group bought the farm, it had no full-time, year-round neighbors closer than two miles away. They found out the place was vacant and for sale because a college buddy from Boston had a weekend getaway cabin down the road apiece. It was never advertised and nobody in the small town where it was located could afford to buy it. Rosie didn't like her late husband's relatives and was determined not to let the property fall into their hands. The group just stumbled onto this opportunity.

There was no real estate agent, no bank, not even an escrow company involved in the purchase. A trusted attorney and judge in town, one Judge Chapman, represented both seller and buyers, handled the escrow, and filed the deed with the county. The farm residents have staged a number of Shakespeare's plays and summer organ concerts in a nearby barn, and a veritable five-foot shelf of published books has been written at the farm, which has been variously called Packer Corners Farm, Total Loss Farm, and Monteverdi Artists Collaborative.

But, you say, nowadays you couldn't buy an old farm from a widow without credit, bank, or escrow company, could you? Of course you can. This case is a perfect example of picking up unwanted rural property in a depressed local economy. Various areas of the U.S. are struggling today with few jobs and declining populations. All you need to find is an older house and a desperate seller somewhere out in the boondocks.

In fact, this kind of living has become more practical with the advent of telecommuting, e-mail, virtual commerce, fax, wireless text messaging, and so on. If your rural home is within even a long commuting distance to your job, and you can work at home some days of the week or send in your work via computer, it could be easier than ever to live in the country and enjoy the peace of nature. Los Angeles executives are willing to drive three hours each way to live in Big Bear up in the mountains, or Idyllwild in the desert, in exchange for much cheaper homes with more living space, better conditions for their children to grow up in, less crime, cleaner air. If you work in Boston, for example, you might be able to live on some pretty country road in New Hampshire and pay a fraction of the cost for a house.

But owner financing is certainly not limited to rural backwaters. Plenty of urban property is distressed and available too, especially if the area in question has suffered from the massive layoffs of manufacturing jobs in the early 2000s, or anytime there is a kind of flight going on. When work is scarce, people have to move on. Seattle, Washington, now a Microsoft boomtown, was virtually a ghost town in the 1970s, after Boeing Aircraft laid off thousands of workers. Every neighborhood had empty houses with assumable FHA mortgages, homes abandoned by people who went elsewhere looking for jobs. "Will the last person to leave Seattle please turn off the lights," said a huge downtown billboard.

Author Ray Mungo and his wife bought a fabulous

large Victorian home with a dazzling view of Lake Union from a young dentist and his wife, who were moving out to a new suburb for more opportunity than Seattle could offer. They paid $20,000 for the house with the dentist himself issuing a wraparound mortgage, since the banks had stopped issuing mortgages and the couple didn't have enough credit. A few years later, and after a divorce, they sold the place for $48,000, cashing out the dentist and splitting the proceeds 50/50. The Seattle economy had picked up some by then, and they'd extensively remodeled and improved the property.

If you really want to find a great owner-will-carry deal, look in areas where other people have been leaving; try to find an area that has innate value and natural resources, a place that will swing back into prosperity eventually. Don't rely solely on the daily newspaper classifieds, although they are invaluable—especially those that specify that the owner will carry. Some people advertise only in smaller weekly or monthly free newspapers, and some just post a sign in the front yard. Drive around to the neighborhoods that interest you on Sunday afternoons. Talk to your friends and coworkers and let them know you're looking for a house the seller will finance. It's surprising how many deals are made between private parties on property that's never been advertised for sale.

NOW, AS EVER, OWNER MAY CARRY . . .
A HISTORY TO TODAY

The times are eternally right for owner financing. The real estate business runs hot and cold, and values tend to go in cycles, although we believe real estate is still the best possible investment you can make. History shows us that no-credit transactions are just as useful, possible, and popular no matter what state the economy might be in, whether it's the inflation-rampant early '80s (interest rates higher than 14 percent were common), the recession of the early '90s, the soaring economy of the late '90s (remember "party like it's 1999"?), or the soft depression and jobless recovery of the early 2000s.

There are several reasons why you will always be able to buy without credit, even when the economy is sound and prices are sky-high. With an assumable mortgage transaction, for example, the seller is interested in getting the difference between the mortgage balance and the sale price, whatever it is. And some sellers will always be willing to carry the mortgage, simply because it is so much more profitable for them in the long run.

In 1978, approximately four million existing single-family homes were sold in the nation. But in 1982, when sales hit rock bottom, fewer than two million were sold. Business was cut in half. Sales gradually crept back up to the four million level by 1989.

In that bleak 1982 season, Dwight and Jane Marshall decided to sell their wonderful adobe home in Santa Fe, New Mexico. Their carefully planned baby turned out to be twins, and they needed a bigger home than the one-bedroom starter home they loved so much. The house was in immaculate condition, only ten years old, and their price was below appraised value, only $55,000! Yet they couldn't find a buyer because the bank mortgage rates were insanely high, somewhere between 12 and 13 percent.

After six months of frustration, they met their perfect buyer. Thirty-five-year-old Anne Marie Fisk was a successful artist who had left her Chicago-area home because she fell in love with the work of Georgia O'Keeffe and the gorgeous New Mexican scenery and creative lifestyle. She was also recovering from a recent divorce and had had a bad falling out with her parents, whom she described as rich but stingy, although an older brother who owned a car dealership had financed a new, baby blue van for her so she could transport her large canvases. For Anne Marie, Santa Fe was a new beginning, a fresh start in life. And the Marshalls' adobe house suited her perfectly. Located on a stunning mesa, it offered views of pink-purple sunsets, and it had a well-lit storage shed that she could turn into a working studio.

Better yet, Anne Marie had landed an artist's job in the graphics department of a slick monthly magazine in town. She didn't have much of a down payment (only $5,000), but between her job and her independent art sales, she seemed easily able to make the monthly payment. The Marshalls gave her a wraparound mortgage for $50,000 at 10 percent and continued to pay their own mortgage on the house, with the provision that Anne Marie would need to get new financing and cash them out in five years, although the mortgage itself was figured as a twenty-year loan. They didn't even check out her credit rating. Her payments were $482.51 a month.

Everything went along swimmingly and everybody was happy for the first eighteen months, until Anne Marie lost her job. Actually, she quit. She claimed the art director was sexually harassing her, but he denied it and the other women in the department were too afraid of losing their jobs to come to Anne Marie's defense. She considered pursuing a court case but gave it up as too much hassle with too much chance of losing. Because she'd resigned voluntarily, she didn't even qualify for unemployment compensation. She wasn't able to find another job in her field because Santa Fe is a fairly small community.

Determined to make it on freelance sales of her art, Anne Marie poured her remaining savings into remodeling the shed as a fabulous working studio. There, she turned out her colorful scenic paintings and began a sideline of hand-designed turquoise jewelry that she took to weekend swap meets all over the Southwest.

It's not easy to make a living as a freelance artist and—you guessed it—before long Anne Marie's mortgage payments started arriving at the Marshalls' house late, then later, then in one-half installments, then not at all.

Dwight and Jane were understanding and patient. Indeed, they liked Anne Marie and wanted nothing more than for her to keep the house and keep up the payments. They even took a small painting in lieu of the mortgage payment one month. But they were still paying their own mortgage on the house and couldn't afford to carry her indefinitely.

The relationship between the Marshalls and Anne Marie became painfully strained. The monthly telephone calls were extremely stressful for both parties.

Things went from bad to worse when Anne Marie's estranged brother in Chicago sent a repossession company to take back the van, which was also behind on its payments. Without the car, she couldn't even get to the swap meets. Then she developed a mysterious and debilitating illness, a kind of allergy so fierce that she had to be rushed to the hospital in the middle of the night, struggling for breath.

The Marshalls couldn't bring themselves to foreclose on Anne Marie in her pitiful condition, but they also couldn't see what alternatives they might have if she continued to be incapable of making her payments. Every now and then, she'd sell a major painting and catch up on her past-due bills, but within a few months she'd be broke again and the unfortunate cycle of late checks and late-night phone calls would begin again.

Despite the problems, the story actually has a happy ending. By 1986, with her five-year balloon payment coming due in less than a year, Anne Marie found the house was worth quite a lot more than the $55,000 she had paid in 1982, and simultaneously the national mortgage interest rates had come down and the real estate picture had brightened, with 3.5 million existing single-family homes sold. She sold the adobe home and studio for a cool $74,900 to a couple from Denver who had good credit and were able to get a bank loan.

The Marshalls got their money out of the house and

paid off their original mortgage, and Anne Marie "walked" with more than $20,000 profit after paying the agent's commission and closing costs. She got a new van and was last seen heading for Colorado.

Everybody won in the end, but if you asked the Marshalls whether they'd ever finance a buyer again, they'd probably say no. It was just too much heartache putting up with Anne Marie Fisk and her freelance art career. But on second thought they might say yes, indeed they would carry owner financing again if times were tough, as in 1982, and they had to do it in order to get a sale. But they'd probably look for a buyer who'd held the same job for at least five years!

THE WORST-CASE SCENARIO, AND THE BEST

At least the Santa Fe artist was honest and hard working. Barney and Joanne Metetsky of Dallas had just about the worst story of seller financing in recent history. They were in the unfortunate position of having to sell a good, solid, two-story house in the Oak Park neighborhood of Dallas in 1987, when the economy of Texas went into a horrible slump.

It was a time when you just plain couldn't sell a house in Dallas without taking a loss, or so it seemed, and the major oil companies were laying off thousands of workers. Barney was out of work himself, but managed to parlay his two master's degrees into a great job as curator of education at a major art museum—in Portland, Oregon. Sadly, Barney and Joanne packed up their belongings and prepared to leave Texas.

They sold the house at a sacrifice. The price was

$96,000, less than the place was worth, and the buyers, Bill and DeeDee Gable, assumed their FHA mortgage of about $70,000, with Barney and Joanne carrying the balance of $26,000 in a second mortgage. That's right, the buyers got the house for nothing down *and* no credit required, and the sellers actually had to pay the agent's commission and closing costs (about $7,000 total) just to get rid of their perfectly nice home in a decent neighborhood.

It got worse. Off in Portland, the Metetskys received their monthly second-mortgage payments (about $260) faithfully and thought nothing was wrong. They didn't realize the Gables were having financial difficulty and had stopped making the first (assumed) mortgage payments until they were notified by the bank that foreclosure was imminent. Hysteria ensued as they tried in vain to reach the Gables, who as it turned out had already left the house abandoned and pretty much trashed. Just to save their credit rating, Barney and Joanne had to pay all the back mortgage payments and put the house up for sale one more time.

By now, you're getting the idea. Seller financing tends to be even more available in times of a depressed economy or when either the property or the seller is in some kind of trouble. But it's also a great vehicle for the seller if the buyer is honest and keeps up the payments. Rosie Franklin never regretted selling the farm in Vermont, and neither did that dentist with the Seattle lakefront house. And here's a contemporary success story worth telling:

Toward the end of the 1990s, when the stock market was soaring, dot-com businesses were making twenty-five-year-old entrepreneurs into overnight millionaires, and real estate in California was red hot, two elderly siblings in Los Angeles took diametrically opposite paths toward retirement security. Jim Takahashi, age seventy-three and retiring from his career as a community college professor, sold his family home in West Hollywood for $450,000 cash and turned the money over to his forty-one-year-old son Barry, who was a high-flying investment analyst for a major New York stock brokerage. Jim figured with the help of his brilliant son, his $450,000 would be four or five million in a couple of years' time, and indeed things went very well at first. In 1999, Barry had his best year. Every month or so, he'd come up with some unknown, obscure little penny stock that would explode in value. Most of them were computer-related, high-technology shares. The nest egg was growing nicely, and Jim was treating himself to chateaubriand, lobster tail, and frequent trips to Las Vegas and Switzerland, with Barry and Barry's girlfriend Vivian. Jim rented an oceanview apartment right on the beach in Marina del Rey.

Jim's sister, Pearl Nomo, age seventy-six, took a different approach. She was a widow whose husband had a successful chain of plant nurseries, and had left her reasonably well-to-do. Their only child, Elaine, was also quite well off and had a thriving career as a corporate attorney in Beverly Hills. Pearl wanted to sell her enormous old house in West L.A. but didn't need the cash, so she carried a first mortgage for a promising young couple in exchange for a serious down payment ($50,000) and a handsome monthly mortgage check

($2,450), and moved into a comfortable two-bedroom apartment in a new seniors' complex downtown. The upkeep was easy, the building had twenty-four-hour-a-day security and assisted-living features such as daily meal service for those who requested it, and the $1,200 rent seemed a bargain for such comfort and safety. The place had a nice view of the city lights and there were always nice neighbors ready for a game of cards or lunch out in a restaurant.

The year 2000 dawned and Barry's career declined. It was insidiously difficult to gauge the market. Whereas he'd once had the Midas touch, turning everything to gold, now Barry's most touted investments started sinking like a rock. Jim's portfolio took heavy losses in the ensuing two years, until by 2002 his original $450,000 was shaved down to $100,000 and still tanking. Panic set in as Barry decided to sell short on the market, essentially betting everything against the stocks, predicting that they would decline further. That didn't work either. Finally, in 2003, the awful truth came out. Jim Takahashi, now seventy-eight, was essentially broke. In five short years since retiring and selling his home for cash, he'd gone from considering himself a wealthy gentleman of leisure to living on a state teacher's retirement pension.

Jim couldn't afford to keep his expensive beach apartment. But fortunately, he wasn't reduced to moving into some hovel. No, in fact he moved in with his sister Pearl downtown. She had the extra bedroom and still had the monthly mortgage check from carrying the sale of her old house. They get along better now than they ever did as younger people, and they like to joke that with modern medical advancements, both expect to live to be one hundred.

That would be practical, since Pearl's monthly checks from selling her house on a twenty-year note will keep coming in until she's ninety-six!

As for Jim, he's one of millions who lost their shirts when the stock market went horribly bad in the early 2000s, and he wishes to heck he'd carried the mortgage on his house rather than plunging into a get-rich-quick program that left him flat. "For now," he says, "I'm just hoping my sister lives forever. At least I've got a place to sleep."

As for you, if you're any kind of sincere buyer, even if your credit is just plain nonexistent, there is definitely a seller out there who's willing to finance you. Don't be afraid to approach sellers with the proposal that they finance the sale. They may turn you down in great consternation, may be insulted by the very notion. But they may also call you back a week or a month later.

You're the buyer. You're in the driver's seat. Just don't take on a payment that you can't realistically meet.

FOUR

Lease with Option

Considering how well it works, and considering that it's so beneficial for both buyers and sellers, it's surprising that the lease with an option to purchase is not used more often. Certainly, it's never lost its appeal. The biggest problem seems to be that most real estate agents hate it. Their attitude is that if you lease with an option to purchase, you still haven't bought the home, and they can't collect their commission. But smart agents know better, as we will demonstrate.

The lease option *is* a form of purchasing, and in many cases it can be done with no credit required. Done properly, it will lead to your owning the home. It's a first step in the door of home ownership, and there are many ways in which it can culminate in a title deed without requiring a visit to the lending officer.

For starters, what is a lease option? It's a contract in which the buyer agrees to rent the house for a specific period of time (usually a year), with all or part of the rent going toward the purchase of the property. Every time you make out a rent check, you increase your equity in the home and improve your chances of buying the place. The lease option contract also establishes the price of the home, so that in essence you have frozen the price.

If, a year later, the property values in the neighborhood have improved and the house is worth more, the seller is stuck with a year-old price, and the buyer gets a bargain. If the value of the home has gone down, however, you're not obliged to exercise your option (buy).

It's a beautiful arrangement. From the seller's point of view, it makes the house much easier to sell, and that's important in a slow or cold market. From the buyer's perspective, it's triply beneficial: it can make a house more affordable, it eliminates the need to qualify for a loan, and it buys some extra time in which to get financing. Indeed, by the time the buyer has paid rent for a year and accumulated equity in the property, a lender may be more inclined to give a mortgage because the buyer has already made the down payment, so to speak. If the buyer has been a good tenant (e.g., always prompt with the rent check), the seller may be persuaded to finance the purchase because he has built up some confidence in the buyer's ability to pay. If the old mortgage is assumable, the seller may be willing to carry a second mortgage.

There is no guarantee that the seller will carry a second mortgage, essentially providing part of the financing, but it makes good sense for a particular kind of seller. If he or she doesn't absolutely need the cash all at one time, there's a lot more profit to be made in extending financing and collecting the interest. Sometimes, too, a seller just doesn't want the hassle of finding a new buyer and will extend you a second mortgage just to complete the sale.

Indeed, some lease option contracts build up so much value that they can actually be sold to another buyer (as long as there is not a clause that prohibits such transfer). The lease option is a kind of ownership because it's a legal, binding guarantee of the right to buy a house at a set price, with a certain amount of equity already paid in.

You'll find only a few homes offered at lease-option terms in newspaper classified ads, but don't be discouraged. Any house for sale may be available for lease option if you make the offer, especially if the home has been sitting unsold for a long time. Even houses for rent could be lease optioned if you can convince the landlord to sell that way.

There is usually (but not always) an option fee, a kind of modest down payment, required to get into a lease-option purchase. This amount, whatever it is, is nonrefundable, so if in the end you don't buy the house, the seller is entitled to keep what you've paid in. Here's a great deal for a buyer without good credit:

Option Fee: $5,000. This is the "$5,000 moves you in" pitch, as we saw with the example of Jim and Shirley Monahan in the introduction to this book. The option payment is completely negotiable and depends on the value of the home. If it's a $250,000 house, five grand might not be enough. The option fee could be more like $10,000. On the other hand, there could be no option fee at all if the house is inexpensive or the seller desperate. We suggest $5,000 as a fair option fee on a house worth less than $200,000. It's a serious enough sum of money to make the seller happy and the buyer motivated. Remember, this amount, if any, is not refundable. But you don't lose it if you buy the house! It goes right toward your purchase, like a regular down payment.

Rent Applied Toward Purchase: $1,500 a month (flexible based on the value of the house, of course). 100 percent applied toward purchase. The 100 percent applied toward purchase would be a terrific deal for any buyer, but not every seller is willing to allow the entire rent to apply. Sometimes they'll offer 75 percent, 50 percent, as little as 25 percent. Like the option fee, it's completely negotiable. As a buyer, you want the largest possible percentage, and preferably *all*, of your rent to go toward the sale price of the house. That way, you're not wasting a penny on rent. You're in effect already paying for the house with every rent check. Paying the full $1,500 a month toward the purchase, in a single year you'd build up $18,000 equity in the home. Add to that the $5,000 option fee, and you've got a $23,000 down payment already made. You're in the neighborhood of a decent down payment on the books, and it's a lot easier to accumulate a down payment with monthly rent than to try to save up such a bundle.

Term of the Option: one year. Some options will go for shorter periods or longer ones, but a year seems about the right amount of time. The seller feels he's not tying up the property for an inordinate amount of time; if you don't buy, he can turn around and resell or re-lease option the house in a year's time, and keep your deposit and rent money. The buyer knows he has a year in which to make sure he really wants to buy the house, to shore up his credit or find new financing, persuade the seller to finance the deal, or perhaps interest a partner or investor into coming in to help out with the purchase.

Renewal of the Option: yes, if both parties agree. There should be a clause that allows for the option to be renewed for a second year, *but* the terms are open to negotiation and may be completely different. For one thing, the seller doesn't have to maintain the price you set in the original contract. He's got every right to increase the price, and is likely to do so if the market has improved or if the house has gone up in value (possibly because of repairs and improvements you've performed while leasing!). The monthly rent could go up also, and the percentage of rent applied to purchase could go down or disappear altogether. If all that sounds rather dire, just be sure to exercise your option and buy the house within the original allotted time. Once the contract expires, all terms are changeable, and you can't expect the average seller to carry a lease option indefinitely. Your best bet: exercise. If you have a good relationship with the seller, however, and that person is not in urgent need of closing the sale, it's possible you could negotiate a second year renewal on agreeable terms.

Transferability of the Option: yes. From a buyer's point of view, it's desirable to have the right to transfer or sell the option to another party, or to invite another investor to share it with you. Not all sellers will go along with this, because they may fear that the new holder of the option will not be reliable, or they may just plain not want to take the chance of dealing with someone they don't know and have never met. But as the buyer you want this power of transferability for some very good reasons. If your option is close to expiring and you still haven't been able to get the financing to close the sale, you could transfer the option to a friend or relative with better credit, let them buy the house, and then sell it back to you. Or, you could find that the option is worth money, quite a lot of money, to another buyer. Let's say you've already put $10,000 into the deal and you've frozen the price at a favorable, low level. Somebody could come along, pay you $10,000 to take over your option, and buy the house for themselves. You got a year's free rent and lost nothing. Maybe you'd even sell the option for $5,000, and get at least half your investment back. Anything is better than losing what you put into the deal just because you can't exercise on time.

If all this exercising sounds like financial aerobics, just remember exercise is good for you! A lease option is like paying rent without losing the rent money. We're not saying you can't lose, because nothing in real estate is foolproof, but if the seller is willing to credit 100 percent of the rent toward the purchase, the buyer almost always exercises his or her option. With every month that passes, the buyer has more invested in the house and more incentive to complete the deal.

(OK, there are exceptions. Ray Mungo lease optioned one of his Seattle fixer-uppers to a couple who got the 100 percent rent credit and loved the house, but didn't buy it in the end because they got a divorce. No matter; he turned around and lease optioned it a second time to another couple.)

Right to Cancel the Lease: The buyer can cancel with thirty days' written notice; the seller should never have the right to cancel the lease, under any circumstances. Some sellers don't want to give the buyers the right to cancel the lease, but most buyers will feel safer and more comfortable with the deal if they have the right to cancel at any time, on a month's notice. The seller, of course, keeps everything paid to him, and can resell or re-lease option the house. You won't cancel the lease if you're happy with the house!

Agent's Commission: Yes, the agent *can* receive his or her commission on a lease-option purchase, and that's something most agents need to understand. One good way to do this is for the seller to give the agent an advance on the commission at the time the lease option is signed, with the balance to be paid when the buyer exercises the option. For example, Jack and Jill sold their house for $130,000 on a lease option, with the buyers putting up a $4,000 option fee. The agent's commission of 6 percent amounts to $7,800 on the sale, so they advance him $1,500 out of the buyer's $4,000 option fee, with $6,300 to follow at closing. The agent was happy to get his first $1,500, Jack and Jill got a $2,500 option fee plus monthly rent, and the buyers got a fabulous deal. If, in the end, they don't buy the house, the agent gets to keep his advance, the sellers get to keep the deposit, plus they get to lease option it again.

The agent in this case learned the valuable lesson that selling a house on a lease option puts money in his pocket and sets up a mechanism that is almost certain to pay his entire commission eventually. This is far better than having the house sit unsold, producing nothing, for months on end while the agency spends money to advertise it, show it, and so forth.

But you'd be amazed at how much resistance some

agents will put up against using the lease option route. We've heard stories of sellers who simply couldn't convince their agent to do it, and had to wait until the listing expired and then do it themselves without an agent, or switch to an agent who would cooperate.

Real estate agents, for the most part, are working for the seller, who pays their commission, so be aware of that. Nonetheless, a savvy agent can be a buyer's best friend! There are just as many different kinds of agents as there are different kinds of people in the world, and it's great when you find an agent you can work with.

Often, a smart agent can literally make the deal happen, even when you lack credit. Also remember that if you find an agent you like, someone who understands your needs, you can use that person as a buyer's agent, a representative who searches out homes that meet your requirements and acts on your behalf with the sellers.

Any well-stocked stationery store will have lease option purchase forms available. The following sample contract is a good, basic one that covers the major points. Add your own clauses to reflect your personal concerns, but if you are going to create original clauses, we strongly advise that you have a competent real estate professional or attorney check your work to be sure that everything about it is legal and proper.

LEASE WITH OPTION TO PURCHASE

RECEIVED FROM _____ (buyers) _____
Hereinafter referred to as Tenant, the sum of _____ dollars
($_____) evidenced by (check one) Cash (   ), Cashier's
Check (   ), Personal Check (   ) as a deposit which, upon ac-
ceptance of this Lease, the Owner of the premises, hereinafter
referred to as Owner, shall apply and deposit as follows:
Nonrefundable option fee: $_____
Rent for the period from _____ to _____ : $_____
Security deposit: $_____
TOTAL: $_____
If Owner does not accept this Lease within three (3) days, this
deposit is to be refunded in full.
Tenant offers to lease from Owner the premises situated in city
of _____ , county of _____ , state of _____ , described
as follows:

_____

_____

on the following terms and conditions:

1. **TERM:** The term shall commence on _____ , 2_____ ,
and continue for a period of _____ months thereafter.

2. **RENT:** Rent shall be _____ dollars ($_____) per
month, payable in advance on the _____ day of the
month to Owner or his authorized agent at the following ad-
dress:_____ , or any other address which Own-
er may specify. In the event rent is not paid within five (5)
days of due date, Tenant agrees to pay a late charge of
$_____ plus 10 percent interest per annum on the over-
due amount. Tenant also agrees to pay $_____ for each
dishonored bank check.

3. **UTILITIES:** Tenant shall be responsible for payment of all utilities and services.

4. **USE:** Premises shall be used as a residence for no more than _____ adults and _____ children.

5. **PETS:** No pets shall be brought onto the premises without prior written consent of the Owner.

6. **TRANSFER OF ASSIGNMENT:** Tenant shall have the right to transfer or assign this agreement or sublet the premises to another party without prior written consent of Owner.

7. **MAINTENANCE AND REPAIRS:** Tenant acknowledges the premises are in good order and repair and Tenant shall at his own expense maintain the premises in a clean and sanitary manner including all equipment, appliances, furnishings and fixtures and shall surrender the same at termination of this agreement in as good a condition as found, except for normal wear and tear. Tenant shall be responsible for any damage to premises as a result of his negligence and that of his family, invitees, or guests. Tenant shall not paint, wallpaper, or otherwise decorate premises without prior written consent of Owner. Tenant shall irrigate and maintain all landscaping, shrubs, lawns, trees, and keep the same clear of rubbish or weeds.

8. **PHYSICAL POSSESSION:** Tenant shall take physical possession of premises within three (3) days of the commencement of term hereof. Tenant shall not be liable for any rent until possession is delivered.

9. **SECURITY DEPOSIT:** Owner may but is not obliged to apply any portion of the security deposit above to Tenant's obligations, with any balance remaining to be refunded to Tenant on termination of this agreement.

10. **ENTRY AND INSPECTION:** Tenant shall permit Owner to enter and inspect premises on reasonable notice for the purpose of making repairs or showing the premises to potential tenants or purchasers.

11. **INDEMNIFICATION:** Tenant agrees to hold Owner blameless for any injury or damage to Tenant or other persons on the premises, unless such injury or damage occurs as a result of Owner's negligence or unlawful act.

12. **DEFAULT:** If Tenant shall fail to pay rent when due or perform any term hereof, after not less than three (3) days' written notice of such default given in the manner required by law, Owner may terminate all rights of Tenant hereunder unless Tenant within said time shall cure such default. If Tenant abandons or vacates the premises while in default of payment of rent, Owner may consider all property left on the premises to be abandoned and may dispose of such property in any legal manner. All property on the premises is hereby subject to lien in favor of Owner for the payment of all sums due. In the event of a default by Tenant, Owner may elect to (a) continue the lease in effect and enforce all his rights and remedies, including the right to recover all rents due, or (b) terminate all Tenant's rights hereunder and recover from Tenant all damages incurred by reason of the breach of this lease.

13. **ATTORNEY'S FEES:** In any legal action brought by either party to enforce the terms hereof, the prevailing party shall be entitled to all costs incurred in such action, including a reasonable attorney's fee.

14. **PEST CONTROL INSPECTION:** The main building and all attached structures are to be inspected by a licensed structural pest control operator prior to delivery of physical possession. Owner to pay for (1) Elimination of infestation and/or infection of wood-destroying pests or organisms, (2) Repair of damage caused by such infestation and/or infection, (3) Correction of conditions which caused said damage. Owner shall not be responsible for any work recommended to correct conditions usually deemed likely to lead to infestation or infection of wood-destroying pests or organisms, where no evidence of actual infestation is found.

15. **HEIRS AND ASSIGNS:** This lease is binding to and continues to the benefit of all heirs, assigns, or successors of the parties herein.

16. **RENTING AFTER EXPIRATION:** After the expiration of this lease, Tenant may continue renting premises with the written consent of Owner on a month-to-month tenancy basis, but no such tenancy after the expiration shall extend the time for the exercise of the purchase option, unless agreed to in writing by Owner.

17. **OPTION:** As long as Tenant is not in default of any terms and conditions herein, Tenant shall have the option to purchase the property herein described at a purchase price of _____ dollars ($_____) on the following terms and

conditions: Nonrefundable option fee of $_____ applies toward purchase, and 100 percent of rent applies toward purchase. Tenant may cancel lease at any time with thirty (30) days' written notice to Owner. If Tenant cancels lease, Tenant cancels the purchase and forfeits the option fee and any rent credits. If Tenant exercises to purchase property, property is to be sold in as-is condition, with no warranties or representations by Owner. Tenant shall receive a copy of the latest pest control inspection report, but Owner shall not pay for any damage whether occurring before or after the date of signing the lease option. Monthly rent must be received by the _____ day of the month or the purchase option becomes void and any rent credit toward the purchase price is forfeited. A second-year lease may be negotiated between Owner and Tenant, with all the terms including purchase price and percentage of rent applied toward purchase negotiable.

(Note: Add here any additional clauses that reflect your personal needs or the needs of the house itself. For example, you might want to have the owner agree to pay for new carpets, or guarantee that certain appliances will stay with the property. The owner may want a clause saying the tenant is 100 percent responsible for the upkeep of the swimming pool or other feature of the house. You or the agent can type in any clause or condition as long as the owner agrees to it.)

18. **ENCUMBRANCES:** Tenant shall take title to the property subject to any existing covenants, conditions, restrictions, reservations, rights of way and easements of record, and any real estate taxes not yet due. The amount of any bond or assessment which is a lien shall be paid by Owner before title is transferred.

19. **PERSONAL PROPERTY:** No personal property on the premises shall be included in the purchase price, with the following exceptions:_____

20. **FIXTURES:** All fixtures permanently attached to the real property shall be included in the purchase price, such fixtures to include all wall coverings, carpets, drapes, blinds, window and door screens, awnings, outdoor plants and trees, and_____.

21. **FINANCING:** The parties acknowledge the impossibility of speculation of availability of future financing. Performance of this agreement shall not be dependent on warranties or representations by broker or Owner of financing. However, Owner agrees to consider any proposal in writing by Tenant requesting full or partial owner financing of the purchase. Owner shall not be obliged to extend any such financing.

22. **TITLE INSURANCE:** Owner agrees to present evidence of title in the form of a title insurance policy prior to Tenant's purchase of the property.
(Note: Title Insurance. The owner should provide the tenant with a copy of his title insurance, just to prove that the title is good and clear. The buyer should also purchase his own title insurance policy.)

23. **EXAMINATION OF TITLE:** Tenant shall have a period of ten (10) days from the date of the exercise of this option to examine the title to the property and report any objections to exceptions to the title. Any exceptions to the title shall be deemed accepted unless Tenant objects in writing within said ten (10) days. If Tenant objects to any exception

to title, Owner shall have sixty (60) days thereafter in which to remove all such exceptions, or if such exceptions are not removed within sixty (60) days, Tenant shall have the right to terminate and end the rights and obligations hereunder unless he agrees to purchase the property subject to such exceptions.

24. **ESCROW AND CLOSING COSTS:** Escrow fees and closing costs shall be entirely paid by Owner.

25. **CLOSE OF ESCROW:** Within _____ days of exercise of the option, Owner and Tenant shall deposit with a valid escrow holder, to be chosen by Owner, all monies and instruments necessary to close escrow and complete the sale of property in accordance with all terms and conditions herein.

26. **PRORATED TAXES AND INSURANCE:** Real estate taxes and insurance premiums on the property are to be prorated between Owner and Tenant as of the date of recording of deed.

27. **EXERCISE OF OPTION:** This option shall be exercised by delivering written notice to Owner prior to the expiration date of this option and by an additional payment on account of the purchase price of $_____ (*Purchase Price minus Option Fee and Rent Credit Paid*) dollars to account of Owner to the authorized escrow holder referred to above. If mailed, the written notice shall be sent by certified mail to Owner at the address above, and shall be deemed to have been delivered on the date of postmark.

28. **EXPIRATION OF OPTION:** This option may be exercised any time after (*month, day, year*) and shall expire at midnight on (*month, day, year*). Upon expiration Owner shall be released from all obligations and all of Tenant's rights shall cease.

The undersigned Tenant hereby acknowledges receipt of a copy of this agreement:

Dated:_____.

_____

Tenant's broker:_____   Tenant:_____

Broker:_____   Buyer:_____

Address:_____   Address:_____

_____   _____

Phone:_____   Phone:_____

Acceptance: The undersigned Owner accepts the foregoing offer:

Broker's fee: Owner agrees to pay (*Broker's name*), the agent in this transaction, _____ percent of the option fee in this agreement and authorizes the agent to deduct said percentage from the deposit received. In addition, Owner agrees to pay on closing of escrow the additional sum of _____ dollars in the event the option is exercised and the sale completed. In the event that legal action is instituted to collect this fee, Owner agrees to pay reasonable attorney's costs.

Dated:_____

_____

Owner's broker:_____   Owner:_____

Broker:_____   Buyer:_____

Address:_____   Address:_____

_____   _____

Phone:_____   Phone:_____

_____

OPTION-AL OPTIMISM

As with our personal real estate contract in the previous chapter, this lease option agreement is a simple
one, with just the essential clauses included. (Some
preprinted option forms are even simpler.) The most
important clauses in our version are clause 6, "Transfer
of Assignment," and clause 21, "Financing." One or
the other of these clauses could help you close the sale
even without adequate credit.

As we mentioned earlier, the ability to transfer or assign the option could be an important factor, because
you could assign it to another party whose credit is
good enough to get a mortgage, and who is willing to
share equity with you, resell the property back to you,
or issue a quitclaim. Your valid option is in itself a kind
of partial ownership with tangible value as long as the
option is exercised before the expiration date.

The financing clause doesn't obligate the seller to finance the purchase, but it does leave that door slightly
open. Here is your chance to establish credit with the
seller even if you have none with the bank. If you pay
your rent on time faithfully, the seller will gradually
come to trust your honesty and ability to pay. After a
year of building up that kind of fiduciary trust, you
may be able to convince the seller to finance the sale or

at least carry some of the paper. A reasonable down payment will help a lot to sweeten the deal.

Sellers and buyers are only human, after all. In many cases, the seller will be so grateful for a lease-option tenant who pays rent on time that he'll do everything possible to make it easier for you to complete the purchase. And you as the tenant have enough time to figure out everything about the house and whether you really want to own it. If you're late on the rent even once, the seller has the right to take away your option and all your rent credit, but many sellers will find the patience to forgive the delay, if you catch up with the rent promptly and have a good excuse for being late. Not every clause has to be rigidly enforced to the letter of the law, but you should not enter into this or any agreement if you're not confident you can live up to its every requirement.

Tenants are often the most likely people to buy a home. For starters, they're already in residence and it's easier to stay put than to move. You're in a great position to buy the home you live in on a lease option if one or more of the following conditions applies:

• The landlord has become a personal friend and decides to sell the house, offering it first to you before putting it on the market.

• You're on a job promotion track that is likely to provide more income in the future than you have now, or you're about to graduate from a professional school with a degree that will lead to new job opportunities.

• You're gradually paying off debts and expect your credit rating to improve in the near future (and you're carefully checking that rating with the three major credit reporting agencies to make sure it reflects your payments).

• The landlord encounters financial difficulties of his or her own, such as medical emergency, divorce, loss of employment, or adverse legal **judgments**.

• The landlord dies and the heirs to the estate need to liquidate the property for tax or other reasons.

• Your parent or relative dies and you suddenly come into a once-in-a-lifetime inheritance, which doesn't have to be huge—just big enough to constitute an irresistible down payment offer to your landlord.

Margaret and Jim Lewis bought their first home in Madison, Wisconsin, just because they happened to be living in it when the owner decided to sell. They never thought they could qualify for a mortgage, with Jim's earnings as an assistant professor at the university being gobbled up each month with little to spare, while Margaret cared for their three children and made a few dollars on the side selling her homemade quilts.

They had one thing going for them, however, when the elderly landlady decided it was time to sell the house. They'd been renting there for almost ten years, and had never been more than a week late paying the rent.

In fact, they were forced to either buy the house or move, and they loved the place so much—and hated the idea of moving all their belongings and maybe having to place the kids in a new school district—that they took out a lease option and decided to at least try their best to complete the sale. The landlady had grown to like Jim and Margaret a lot and even considered their children as surrogate grandchildren for whom she baked cookies and sent birthday cards.

The lease option required no option fee at all, and their rent went up only $100 a month, but Jim and Margaret had only a year in which to finance the purchase. They found an astonishing motivation in the simple fact that every rent check was increasing their down payment. Jim found that the credit union open to employees of the university was far more liberal than any conventional bank lender, and Margaret took a job as a cashier in the campus bookstore to supplement their income. But in the end—with just a month to spare—they squeaked by and got the credit union home mortgage. The union officer told Jim it was possible only because the lease option had given them a substantial down payment, and locked in a great price, so that the house itself was worth 30 percent more than the loan. (See chapter 5, "The 30/70 Rule.")

Jim and Margaret's experience shows one way in which a rental property can be turned into a lease option purchase. Taking a page from their book, you can forget about the houses listed for sale and instead go out looking at houses for rent. Find a rental you like and offer the landlord to lease option it. You have nothing to lose, and you'd be surprised at the number of landlords who might be interested.

Charlie Merriweather, a newly single guy in his thirties, had an otherworldly experience with rental-turned-option in Sacramento, California. Divorced and desolate, he was sleeping on a friend's couch, his belongings locked in a public storage place, when he met someone he came to call the Mad Rabbi in the religion section of a bookstore. They struck up a conversation about the Old Testament. Although Charlie wasn't particularly religious, the pain of divorce had simply sent him running into the arms of any spiritual consolation he could find.

At any rate, after some soul-searching talk, the Mad Rabbi asked Charlie where he lived, and after hearing the sad tale of his sudden homelessness, offered to rent Charlie a small house in the north end of town with an option to purchase it.

This was some kind of bolt from the blue, not likely to happen to anyone, but nonetheless a true story. Charlie investigated the house and found it was a fabulous 1930s Sacramento bungalow with fireplace, carpets, upstairs bedrooms for the kids, a fenced backyard with a fish pond, and leaded glass windows, on a very busy street but set back seventy-five feet from the sidewalk. It was a great place for a noncustodial parent, and it was clean, the heat was on, the refrigerator cold, and the gas range operational. The "mad" thing about the house, and the reason Charlie called the rabbi the "Mad Rabbi," was that the property had been sitting there empty, unrented, and not actively for sale, for more than a year, with full utilities on and a cleaning lady coming over now and then. There was no key to the house, but you could get in by entering through the back door or the garage.

The rabbi owned dozens of little houses; they made him feel secure. He never advertised them, just waited for the right person to come along. He specialized in helping down-and-out people who had enough resources to pay the rent. The deal he offered Charlie was $550 a month to accrue over a year to a down payment of $6,600, after which time Charlie could buy the house for about $40,000 with the rabbi's financing (mid-1980s prices).

It was a deal made in heaven all right, with the full blessing of the prophets, but Charlie blew it. He started drinking heavily, fell behind in the rent, lost the confidence of the rabbi (who was definitely "mad" when he didn't get his check), and eventually packed everything he could carry into his car and left Sacramento for some place—anyplace—where he could start a new life. Divorce will do that to people.

But before leaving the house, Charlie turned the place over to a family of four, friends who had been looking for a place to rent. He didn't have any authority to let other people live in the house, but he knew this family was responsible and would pay the rent promptly, and since they were also Jewish he figured the rabbi would like them. Astonishingly enough, it worked out well. The family took over the house and the lease option, always paid the rabbi on time, and, so to speak, lived happily ever after.

Lease option deals aren't limited to low-cost, old, or

unwanted properties. In late 2003, we are finding homes offered for lease option approaching a half million dollars or more. Author Robert Yamaguchi encountered such a gem while walking around his neighborhood of Signal Hill, California, a small city located within the boundaries of much-larger Long Beach. Robert bought an oceanview condominium in Signal Hill in 1997 from the estate of a dead man (see chapter 10, "*En Viager*: Buying from the Old, Dying, and Dead") for $127,000. The unfortunately deceased seller was in debt over his head and his heirs, desperate to settle his estate, just wanted someone to take over the payments. Six years later, in 2003, the condo was appraised at $320,000—an astonishing increase in value over a short time.

Much of that lucky appreciation in value is simply due to what happened in Signal Hill. Developers came in and transformed what had been a working class, oil well–studded, rough-and-tumble neighborhood of Long Beach into a lush paradise of brand-new, single-family homes connected by landscaped trails and pocket parks leading to a hilltop sculpture simulating the Native Americans' practice of sending smoke signals out to sea and Catalina Island. The new houses sell from $650,000 to $1 million dollars each, and hundreds of them were sold even before construction was complete.

The new wealthy community in Signal Hill had a dramatic impact on the prices and value of adjoining, existing homes such as Robert's modest two-bedroom condo. Every house and condo in the town doubled to tripled in value in only six years. So here's the deal a creative seller was offering in a handmade flyer: would you go for it? Bruce is looking to sell his three-bedroom, four-bathroom, three-story condo with two balconies and beautiful ocean and city views on a lease option *and* with seller financing. He suggests a lease option with $15,000 down (nonrefundable option payment) and rent of $2,450 a month over *two* years. He is also willing to carry a second mortgage to help with the financing. The asking price is $459,000.

Robert knew quite well that this condo was worth about $150,000 six years ago, and that $459,000 in 2003 was probably stretching its value to the absolute limit. But Bruce, the seller, in giving a buyer two years on a lease option, is essentially selling the future value of the place. In other words, you could fix the price today and, if home prices in Signal Hill continue their breathless ascent, by the time you had to exercise the option, the place might be worth $600,000 or even more. Any mortgage lender would be happy to finance the sale for a home worth more than $600,000 when the original purchase price of $459,000 has been diminished by a $15,000 down payment and two years of $2,450 rent payments ($58,800). The buyer holding the option would have developed a healthy 33 percent equity by exercising, and lenders observe the "30/70 rule" as described in chapter 5, even for buyers with bad credit.

There is even a prospect for a quick and profitable flip in this deal. Just before the option is about to expire, you could line up a new buyer, exercise your option and buy the place for less than $400,000 owed, and turn around and sell it for $600,000 or more on the same day or very shortly after, and walk away with a $200,000 profit on top of having your two years of rent reimbursed to you.

If it sounds too good to be true, maybe it isn't. That is, you are taking a risk. Nobody can say for sure that real estate values in any given town are going to continue to soar 25 percent a year, simply because they've been doing that recently. What if values in Signal Hill should stagnate? What if they should go down? What if Boeing Aircraft shuts down its Long Beach plant or the city goes through one of its periodic down cycles of unemployment? Exactly ten years earlier, in 1993, Signal Hill was scraping the bottom of the barrel, as condo prices plunged so badly that people abandoned their homes because they owed more than they could sell for. Robert's own next-door neighbor walked away from her condo, leaving it occupied by her heavily tattooed, much pierced, twenty-year-old grandson and his band of young friends, who squatted there for six months without paying a dime, playing their CDs and having loud parties until the foreclosure process forced them out.

But somebody will take a chance on Bruce's lease option offer, for sure. Property in Signal Hill is hot, buyers are tripping over themselves to "get in," and someone could very likely make a decent profit on the investment, or at least a decent home.

Let's look at an earlier luxury condominium story. When Carolyn Yamamoto was having trouble selling her plush condo in the Hollywood hills in 1990, she finally succeeded by leasing it with an option. The place had a swimming pool, shared by six apartments, with a breathtaking view of Los Angeles from the San Bernardino Mountains to the sea. There was an eight-person hot tub, a laundry room, and secured parking under the building, plus her apartment featured cathedral ceilings, two fireplaces, two baths, and a dazzling view from the living room, formal dining room, and modern kitchen. Everything about this condo was luxurious and modern. The price was $189,000, exactly what Carolyn herself had paid for it two years earlier.

But after all that, it had only one bedroom, and the rules of the condo association prohibited children and dogs. Carolyn was up against the age-old problem that most buyers don't want a one-bedroom condo. The type of people who buy a home usually need more space than that and frequently have children. She needed a special buyer, and after months of frustration with no sale, she found Randy and Jamie, a middle-aged couple with two cats, who lease optioned the condo for $1,200 a month with no option fee, but they did pay an extra month's rent in advance as a security deposit.

That deal worked out fine for everyone. Carolyn was able to move on to her new job in San Francisco, while Randy and Jamie took good care of the condo and in fact became popular hosts in the building, getting along well with the other condo owners. Their credit was shaky, but after a year they managed to swing a mortgage with a down payment borrowed from Randy's parents, because they effectively paid less for the condo than it was worth three years earlier when it was brand new.

That tells you something about condos, by the way.

Compared with single-family homes, they do not usually appreciate much in value—Robert's experience in Signal Hill was an exception to the rule. You can't add rooms or remodel/redesign a condo to increase its worth as you can with a detached house. You have to put up with the regulations imposed by a homeowners' association, which can get downright nasty and political and limit or restrict everything you want to do, from the color of your exterior paint to the nocturnal habits of your cat. Most people want a single-family home, not an apartment, when they buy real estate, but condos make sense if you live in a major urban area or you're retired and tired of maintaining a yard or big house, or if you're simply a busy person who hates housework.

You can also regard a condo as a starter, just something to get out of renting and into real property until you can roll over (IRS lingo for selling your home and buying another) into a real house. And condos are available on a lease option basis, no credit required, in virtually every city in the nation. Some are even nothing down, "just take over payments." Many condo dwellers are perfectly happy with their units and have no particular desire to trade up to a house. "Home sweet home" is a highly personal choice.

FIVE

The 30/70 Rule

It's not really a rule, or at least we haven't been able to find it written down anywhere, and no banker would admit to it as a hard-and-fast guideline, but it's a common practice in lending circles that if you can put 30 percent of the price of a house as a down payment, the lender will issue a mortgage for the remaining 70 percent, even if you don't have enough credit.

The reasoning is simply that anyone who pays 30 percent into a house is highly unlikely to walk away from the investment. It's a real commitment, and eliminates the necessity of a good credit rating. And if the bank or lender should be forced to foreclose on the mortgage, presumably the house will be worth a great deal more than the amount owed on it.

Of course, the house itself has to be worth the amount of the sale price, or this practice would be meaningless. The bank or lending agency will insist on valuing the property through a professional assessment or **appraisal**. The appraiser will look at the physical condition of the property and also take into account the comparables, the prices recently paid for similar property in the same vicinity. Once the value of the home is established and you're able to put 30 percent or more of that value down, you should be able to get a mortgage even if you've had past credit problems or have no credit at all.

There is no better example of this than our old friend Patty Callahan in Cambria, California. Patty would be the first to admit that her credit was just plain awful. She had a drinking problem in her twenties and thirties, which she has since recovered from completely, and she is a sober and proud attorney specializing in family and child custody disputes.

But when Patty arrived in Cambria from her childhood home in Seattle, she was young and a little wild. She had a daughter out of wedlock and decided to raise the child herself, which wasn't easy on the salary of a substitute schoolteacher, her profession at the time. Patty and baby moved into a bohemian cabin in the woods along the Big Sur coastline during a time when such digs could be had cheaply. They raised chickens and dozens of other animals in a horribly unkempt yard—and seemed to live on the sun in the morning and the moon at night. That, and large quantities of frozen vodka.

Inside, the house was the messiest place anyone had ever seen, even in disheveled Big Sur circles. Patty hung a wooden sign reading DISORDERLY ROOM over her mantel. She never did the dishes until there was nothing clean left to eat on or drink from. Laundry was tossed on the floors, in heaps. She lavished love and attention on her child, however, and the little girl was never neglected. The Callahan gals had a free and easy lifestyle.

When Patty needed money, she'd simply write a check, whether or not there were funds in her account.

She bounced checks all over the central coast until she was kicked out of every bank in town and even the teachers' credit union. Those few establishments foolish enough to give Patty a credit card soon came to regret it. She ran up massive debts in restaurants, clothing stores, and liquor stores until the cards were repossessed, and never bothered to make a payment. She was not a thief and not dishonest, and eventually had to repay every one of the bad checks and credit card bills. She was just a young person who had no sense of responsibility about money.

Finally, Patty met the person she'd needed all along to keep her on the straight and narrow path. The kindly Mrs. Chin, a professional bookkeeper, agreed to take over Patty's financial affairs for nothing more than love and affection for Patty and her daughter. After that, all Patty's salary went directly to Mrs. Chin, who in turn paid Patty's bills and doled out small amounts of cash for Patty's gas and liquor expenses. Patty was not allowed to write a check or use a credit card. In time, the bills got paid, but her credit rating was still a disaster. The mere mention of Patty's social security number would set every computer in California to screaming, beeping red lights.

If you knew Patty's background, all of this was even more bizarre. Her father was a wealthy and prominent doctor in Seattle. Her siblings were all doctors, lawyers, and CEOs. The family was respectable as could be, social register types. They lavished gifts on Patty's young daughter, who always had new clothes and toys and good health care, but they wouldn't give Patty any actual cash because they knew she'd blow it. She was the rebel, the black sheep of the family. Every few years, her father would give her a car, but hold the title himself so she couldn't sell the vehicle. She drove in California for twenty years with Washington state license plates.

Patty was about forty when her father died. Her mother had already passed away, and each of the doctor's children came into a substantial inheritance.

This was the moment, financially speaking, Patty had been waiting for. Without batting an eyelash, she picked out a gorgeous $300,000 home in an upper middle class neighborhood of Cambria and walked into a bank with a down payment of $100,000 in a cashier's check. She got the mortgage, of course, despite her disastrous credit history, and overnight went from being a hippie in a cabin to a law student in a handsome five-bedroom, three-bath Cambria charmer.

The new house didn't make Patty a better housekeeper, but she finally could afford to have a cleaning lady come in twice a week. She rented out her extra bedrooms and her little studio in the backyard to fellow law students, seasonal visitors, any decent tenant who would help her with the mortgage payments. Of course, Mrs. Chin still wrote the checks. And—you guessed it—merely owning the fine house gave Patty excellent credit!

You don't have to inherit money to buy a house on the 30/70 rule, but some kind of windfall like that certainly helps, and a lot of people do experience a once-in-a-lifetime financial boost. Maybe you'll win the lottery, or have a highly successful business project. But a bank will be a good deal more impressed if you save that 30 percent down payment through regular and methodical savings.

"The underlying principle is that a bank's perceived risk is higher with a person who doesn't have good credit," says Lynne Susman Ballew, vice president of the Tokai Bank in San Diego, a lender that provides home financing. "But if they look at you and you've managed to save up a 30 percent down payment, they may say, 'Well, the buyer doesn't have credit but they've saved a lot of money,' and issue the mortgage.

"Is the 30/70 rule a practice? Well, yes, it's a practice but it's not a rule so much as it's just basic banking sense," she continues. "The bank will look at the house itself, and if the bank is interested in investing in that property, it may issue the loan even though the buyer's credit isn't excellent. A person with very good credit can get a 90 percent loan. But a 70 percent loan or lower is considered safe because if it ever had to repossess the property, the bank figures it could get its money back.

"Of course, the bank is going to look at everything more closely because of the buyer's lack of credit. That's part of the perceived-risk factor," Ballew adds. "But when you ask if a person can get a 70 percent loan despite bad credit, I'd have to say yes—sometimes."

For the sake of easy numbers, let's assume the house you want to buy costs $100,000, so the down payment you'd need to employ the 30/70 rule is $30,000. Short of robbing a bank, where could you get $30,000? Joking aside, this is exactly the way most people would implement a 30/70 no-credit purchase: determine the down payment needed, then find a way to raise it. If you have generous parents or good friends who can afford it, you could perhaps borrow the down payment on your personal good name. Be advised, though, that a bank or lender will not be pleased to learn that you have borrowed the down payment, especially if you have signed a note promising to repay it on some established schedule.

It's far better if the down payment comes from a source—any source—that doesn't require repayment, such as inheritance, savings, selling your prized antique classic automobile, cashing in some stock, gambling winnings (why not?), a huge insurance settlement or lawsuit proceeds, or just an outright gift.

Remember, there's no law saying that you must divulge where you got the money, but on the other hand it's definitely illegal to misrepresent your finances in a fraudulent way. So if you have indeed borrowed the down payment and signed a promissory note, you must disclose that. More than likely, that loan will also be a lien against the property in case you can't repay it, much like a second deed of trust. In a case where you borrow the down payment of 30 percent and then borrow the remaining 70 percent from a bank or lender, you're in effect getting 100 percent financing. It happens.

Parents, living or dead, are probably the most likely source of cash for a down payment. That's because many young adults can no longer afford to buy that first home without some help. But gifts or loans from parents aren't always advisable and don't always go smoothly, so beware. Just read "Dear Abby" and other

advice columnists for firsthand accounts from estranged parents who loaned their children money,
never got repaid, and came to resent it. Brothers and
sisters will also sometimes become resentful if a parent
gives a large real estate down payment to one child
while not offering equal amounts to the siblings.

But parents usually want to see their children do
well, and if you're lucky enough to have parents willing
and able to help you buy a home, consider yourself
blessed.

It's good to know, in any case, that if you can some-
how scrape up a 30 percent down payment, your lack
of credit should not stand in the way of buying a home.

SIX

Adverse Possession

It takes only five years in California, but a full thirty years in Texas, to gain legal title to property through adverse possession, a kind of legal theft sometimes referred to as squatter's rights. Every state has adverse possession laws, so check with your state's Department of Real Estate for the requirements in your vicinity.

Adverse possession is simply the acquisition of real estate by occupying it and paying the property tax on it. If it seems incredible that anyone could gain property that way, be assured that it happens thousands of times every year.

Not only is no credit required, but no payments to the previous owner are required, either. Adverse possession is like squatting except that it's legal and you eventually get title.

This works mostly with real estate that has been abandoned by its rightful owner. Adverse possession laws exist on the books to encourage property to be used, not sit vacant. Of course there are stringent rules that must be followed and all states require that your adverse use of the property must be:

- Open

- Continuous, for the minimum number of years in your state

- Notorious—in other words, obvious

- Hostile, which simply means without permission from the owner

- Exclusive, that is, not sharing with other people

- And, you *must* pay the property taxes, even if someone else is also paying them. If there is an existing mortgage on the house that no one else is paying, then you must pay that too, of course, or the mortgage holder will get the property in foreclosure. But paying the mortgage is not one of the legal requirements for adverse possession, whereas paying the taxes is.

After meeting all these conditions, you can then sue in state court and be granted full title, even though you haven't paid for the house and have no credit.

Most successful adverse possession occurs in remote rural areas, where the rightful property owner may forget about or simply ignore his real estate for years. But there are also cases on record where urban property in major cities changes hands through adverse possession.

So where do you find these free houses? You look for property that has clearly been abandoned for one reason or another. Perhaps the owner is serving a long jail term in Mexico, or has moved to another state following a bitter divorce, or has suffered amnesia or Alzheimer's and is wandering around the back streets of a major city with other homeless people. Anything is possible. Some property owners are simply eccentric, mentally ill, senile, or have no one to protect their interests. Some owners literally forget that they own the property and can't be found, no matter how hard you try.

In any case, once you find a house that's clearly unoccupied and abandoned, the law permits you to move in, start paying the taxes, and begin your waiting term of adverse possession. You don't even need to contact the owner, *but* if the rightful owner appears or contacts you and orders you to leave the premises, you have no right to stay. In short, all an owner has to do to protect himself against adverse possessors is to check his property, or have a representative check it, once in a while.

We've seen adverse possession work successfully twice, both times in California. One house was a crack cocaine "shooting gallery," a drug haven abandoned by its owners to tough street gangs in East Los Angeles. Brave neighbor Dave Santiago moved in, fought off the gangs, and claimed the house on Shamrock Street for his growing family. Who wants an abandoned drug den? you might well ask, but the other case was a truly handsome oceanfront home in Pacific Grove, a dilapidated Victorian that was crumbling away but had inherent value because of its superb architecture and location close to the beach. The owner was a stubborn old man living in a wilderness trailer in Watsonville, who received mail at a post office box and utterly refused to do anything about the vacant house. Before adverse possession, the Australian couple who wound up getting the property had written to the owner and attempted to rent or buy the house, but he never replied and never visited the place. One stormy night, they just moved into the house rather than sleep on the beach. They figured they had nothing to lose.

You *can* lose in adverse possession, of course. Suppose you've been living in the house, paying the taxes, for four and a half years. In that time, you've spent thousands of dollars fixing up the place, installing new hardwood floors, replacing the leaky roof, and so forth. The rightful owner can come back from the dead, or Baghdad, or wherever, and reclaim his house and you would have no rights to it. Your investment would have been wasted (although you did get free rent for years).

If adverse possession is risky, it is also tantalizing. Imagine owning a house for practically nothing, only the taxes, just by taking it over! To enhance your eligibility, make sure you keep meticulous records and can prove the five major points:

- **Open.** Your occupancy must be open; it cannot be secretive. The Australian couple on the beach lived in the house without curtains or shades on the living room windows, so that any passersby could observe them when they were sitting in their living room, enjoying the splashy ocean views. Dave Santiago in East L.A. kept lights burning in his front windows all night.

- **Notorious.** This takes "open" a step further. It just means that your occupancy is obvious and blatant. Park your car in the driveway, sit on your rocker on the front porch, receive mail, open utility accounts, have a phone listed in your own name at your adverse address.

• **Continuous.** You can't get title if you've moved back and forth from the house. You must stay there more or less all the time, keeping it as your only principal residence, for the minimum number of years your state requires.

• **Hostile.** You must *not* have the owner's permission to stay in the house. If you're staying there with permission, you will never qualify to own the house by adverse possession. Curiously, the best way an owner can protect himself from losing title to adverse possessors is to simply give them permission to occupy the place, a permission he can later rescind at any time.

• **Exclusive.** This simply means that one individual or family occupies the property—it's not a public crash pad open to all comers.

• **Pay the taxes.** The taxes assessed on real property are a matter of public record. You can find out how much the taxes are on your adverse address, then pay that amount to the county when due. Keep receipts and records of every payment. There have been cases of people who adversely occupied property for twenty years or more but could not gain title, because they didn't pay the taxes. The original intent of this law was to keep property taxes coming in to the government.

Finally, after you have met all these conditions, go to court and sue for **quiet title**, so named because it passes from the previous owner to you quietly, without the former owner being notified.

Many an owner has been startled or distressed to discover that his real estate no longer belongs to him. It has been stolen by adverse possession, and this kind of theft is completely legal and above board. Once the title has been transferred by the court, the property belongs to the adverse possessor forever, until he or she sells it, passes it along to heirs or assigns, or loses it by neglect to the next adverse possessor to come along!

Although most real estate transactions don't require the services of a lawyer, adverse possession is one area in which you can't be too careful. Get a competent real estate attorney to handle your documentation.

AN ONGOING ADVERSARIAL AFFAIR

A small house on Polk Street in San Francisco has been driving real estate agents crazy for years. Some creative soul took an ordinary two-bedroom cottage and remodeled it to resemble the pyramids of Egypt, with a conical roof line and a burnt umber paint job. The house is either hideous or wonderful, depending on your taste, but it's certainly unusual, and everyone who gets past the thick bushes in the front yard to see it has some comment about it.

At one time, the owner, a single man in his forties,

put it up for sale, but the real estate listing expired after four months. The agency is not allowed to sell the house without a current listing, but the owner simply disappeared. Letters to his last known address are returned. His last phone number is disconnected.

Years have passed and a number of brave buyers have wanted to purchase the house, but couldn't. Finally, a radical coalition of activists for the huge homeless population in San Francisco decided to conduct a formal adverse possession of the property as an overnight shelter for street people. But it's unknown whether they will be able to prove their use is exclusive, since a group of people share the space. They will argue that the coalition itself, a nonprofit corporation, is the exclusive adverse possessor.

The most notorious example of adverse possession was also in San Francisco, as described by real estate columnist Robert J. Bruss. Thomas W. Stevens went to the California Supreme Court to argue his claim that he had adversely occupied an apartment building at 1899 Oak Street in the Haight-Ashbury district (*Stevens v. Tobin*, 251 Cal.Rptr. 587). He met the criteria for his occupancy being open, hostile, exclusive, notorious, and continuous. But he still lost the quiet title lawsuit because he didn't have proof that he'd paid the taxes.

PRESCRIPTIVE EASEMENTS

Another, less dramatic form of adverse possession is the prescriptive **easement**, in which the owner of the property loses rights to it by not preventing someone else from using it over a number of years. The classic example is the neighbor who regularly walks or drives across your property to get to his own. If he does so without permission for the required number of years, he could get a prescriptive easement giving him the right to use that land.

This kind of thing also comes up in fence and border disputes. If your neighbor puts up a fence that is actually twelve inches over on your side of the property line and you don't complain about it, he could eventually own a prescriptive easement on that extra foot of territory.

Prescriptive easements are another way of acquiring real estate without credit. Columnist Robert J. Bruss tells the story of a friend who tried to buy a vacant lot adjacent to his property, but the out-of-state corporation that owned the lot "demanded an outrageous price." So Bruss's friend "had the property paved as a parking lot and is earning income from it. He's also paying the property taxes. After the required number of years, he will sue the owner in a quiet title action to obtain the title by adverse possession."

Adverse possession offers the possibility of the whole ball of wax—a house that is yours for the taking. Find a ghost town out in the wild West, a burned-out brick town house in the central city, or just some eccentric property that has been left vacant and unattended, and you could be in. At any rate, there's no landlord demanding rent.

How can it be that easy? Well, it's not, really. Adverse possession takes a number of years to culminate in a legal transfer of ownership and includes a lot of risk. It's not easy, but it's possible. Remember, however:

• **A vacant house is not necessarily abandoned.** The truly abandoned property is a rarity. You don't want to be charged with trespassing on someone else's property. Before even thinking of taking adverse possession of a house, you should make every effort to locate the rightful owner. If such a person can be found, the chances are slim to none that he or she will allow you to take title by adverse possession. With most successful adverse possessions, the property is literally abandoned.

(It can sometimes be a challenge finding the rightful owner of a vacant property. You can contact the county tax collector, where it is a matter of public record to list the address where the tax bill is sent. You can research the death records in the area to determine whether an owner may have died. And you can look into probate court records to see if a deceased owner's estate has been placed in probate.)

• **The laws vary from state to state.** Look into the regulations in your state by contacting the state Department of Real Estate or asking a competent professional Realtor or attorney.

• **Keep impeccable records and stay within the law.** The law may allow you to take adverse possession, but if the rightful owner asks you to leave, you have no right to stay.

SEVEN

Equity Sharing

It's back! Not that it ever went away. Equity sharing was the newest trend in real estate in the inflation-plagued 1980s, but it makes even more sense in the 2000s where some areas are seeing record-high prices. It's a fine way to acquire property without adequate credit to qualify for a mortgage. Equity sharing is simply the sharing of the ownership of real property among several parties.

You will find Equity Share as a category in the classified listings in places where home values have gone through the roof. A typical ad will read, "NO QUALIFY! Stop wasting your money on rent. Make the mortgage payment on new and resale houses throughout the area, receive 50% ownership, plus tax benefits with zero down. Call Broker xxx-xxxx." But the great majority of these types of deals occur between people who already know each other, like family, friends, or coworkers.

Too good to be true? The good news is that it works, at least for some people some of the time. A few examples:

1. One party puts up the down payment and credit, while the other invests sweat. In this case, an investor with good credit and some cash on hand swings the purchase, while the person without credit or a down payment actually lives in the house, fixes it up, and pays 100 percent of the mortgage payments. It's called sweat equity because these houses are usually fixer-uppers that both parties have agreed will be renovated and, eventually, resold at a profit.

Done right, this system works beautifully. You need to find a house that is cheap because it needs work, in a neighborhood that is decent and likely to improve in value. Often, the work involved is merely cosmetic—paint, wallpaper, carpets, landscaping, cleanup, and basic repairs. If the house needs fundamental constructive work such as foundation repair, a new roof, or replacement plumbing or electricity, you're almost certainly going to need professional help, and you should find out in advance exactly what it's going to cost.

Of course, you also need to find an investor rich enough (and smart enough) to put up the down payment and qualify for the mortgage. Certain real estate brokers now make a specialty of marrying these investors with good sweat-equity folks who can be counted on to make the mortgage payment and enhance the value of the property.

Why would an investor want to do this? There are some excellent reasons, and none better than the prospect of a whole lot better return than he could ever get from a bank savings account, stock purchase, or other investment tool. There are many possible tax advantages that may be attractive to a person in an upper-income bracket. Doctors are well known for their real estate investments. More important than the tax advantage, however, is the eventual (and perhaps tremendous) profit. And all the while, the investor doesn't have to do a lick of work or make a single mortgage payment.

The investor and the sweat-equity buyer must come to a formal agreement that the property will be resold in a specific number of years. Three to five years is a good standard, because it typically takes that long for a house to appreciate in value significantly, although some people turn a property around in only a year or two.

When the home is sold, both the investor and the sweat-equity owner/occupant should come away with a tidy profit. That money, plus the fact that you've been making regular mortgage payments for several years, will likely improve your credit situation quite a bit. Even if it doesn't, you will have effectively gotten a start in home ownership, stopped paying rent, picked up the mortgage interest tax deduction, and made your own work and monthly payments produce a return for you, instead of the landlord.

Half a loaf *is* better than none!

2.   Both parties occupy the property in a shared living arrangement. This works best with a duplex, where each party in the equity sharing arrangement has a private and equally good place to live, but the possibilities are endless. Perhaps the house has a granny unit, or mother-in-law apartment, or a small studio cottage in the backyard. One investor, the one who put up the greater share of the down payment, could live in the house, while the other lives in the smaller unit.

Or perhaps one party puts up the entire down payment while the other puts up his or her good credit to qualify for the mortgage, then both parties pay equal shares of the monthly payment.

Everything is negotiable with a shared living arrangement, including the percentage of equity and monthly payment. If you live in the tiny backyard cottage while the other party gets the big four-bedroom house, you might realistically be expected to pay less or to own a smaller percentage of the property.

A shared living arrangement makes sense in any market where real estate has become too expensive for the majority of people. In California in 2003, only 37 percent of people were rich enough to afford the median cost of a home, meaning 63 percent of the population couldn't. The statistics on housing affordability are frightening, and getting worse every year. But if you're going to share living quarters with another buyer, naturally you must be sure that you can get along. If you go to bed early and lead a quiet life, you might not be happy with neighbors who party noisily till dawn. It's best to find out as much as possible about your partners before entering into a shared living situation.

3. The seller becomes your equity partner. This really is the wave of the future and is happening right now in every part of the country. When a seller is desperate to get out from under a mortgage payment and the house hasn't sold, it may be to his advantage to sell 50 percent equity in the property to any buyer who will take over the payments. Usually, the deal is cut for a period up to five years, after which you must either buy out the seller or resell the home and split the proceeds.

There is rarely a cash down payment involved, and absolutely no qualifying credit is required, but the seller may insist that you pay the closing costs and the agent's commission, since the seller is getting no money up front and can't be expected to actually pay money to sell his home.

You don't need a new mortgage because you just pay the seller's existing mortgage payment, based completely on his or her credit. Sometimes this will give you a low monthly payment because it's an older mortgage. More often, it's a recent mortgage and a high payment that somebody can't handle because of job loss. Of course you're buying only half the house, and half the equity, and within three to five years you must refinance, buy out your partner, or sell and move on.

You acquire a house where the seller gets only the relief from making payments, and won't see his cash-out for years to come. So you need to find a seller whose back is to the wall, someone who has already moved or who simply can't afford to make the payments. Sellers like that are more common in times of high unemployment. Their misfortune could be your door to home ownership.

Remember, however, that you're buying only half the house while paying the full mortgage payment, and that within five years your back could be to the wall, too, if you can't sell or refinance the house. Try to find something with an excellent prospect for improving in value.

4. Group purchase, or *hui* plan. Sometimes a group of people get together and buy property on which some of them may live, whereas others simply hold an investment share. You find this frequently in Hawaii, where this kind of group is called a hui, because land values are staggeringly high and the smallest "little grass shack" might be worth millions.

There are endless variations on group purchasing. The "back to the land" movement of the late 1960s and 1970s saw a large number of communes formed by groups who bought houses and land in rural areas and lived there together. Many people thought communes were a radical idea, but actually such intentional communities have long existed in American history, including among the Shakers and the Amish.

A modern adaptation is a corporation, a nonprofit membership association formed to purchase real estate. Each member holds stock in the corporation and a share of the property. The stock can be sold to another party, but usually the corporation bylaws will insist on membership approval of any new person joining the group, or you may be required to offer to sell your stock back to the corporation and its members before offering it to anyone else.

The group purchase can be an excellent way for you to get at least a piece of real property ownership without needing personal credit. Typically, the corporation or group is granted the mortgage, not the individual investors. If you expect to live on the property, that arrangement must be in writing and absolutely specific.

The ideal group purchase situation might be in a rural setting where there is plenty of land and enough houses for everyone who wants to have a personal domicile, but the same principle can applied to urban living through membership cooperatives. Some co-op apartment buildings in New York City and other major urban hubs have been doing it successfully and profitably for years.

In a way, a condominium building is a kind of group ownership, with membership association and communal upkeep fees, but when you buy a condo, you are buying a particular and individual space, and some credit is usually required to qualify for the mortgage. In a true group purchase, your personal credit is not the foundation for the loan. In short, if you have some good friends who are as eager as you are to stop paying rent, get your group together and buy! Many hands make light work, and you could be amazed at the power of numbers. Just be sure you really like the others, and have an inviolable personal living space guaranteed.

5. Time-share. Time-share properties are usually in resort areas, and your investment buys only a few weeks a year of residential privileges. It's certainly a form of equity sharing, because you can sell the property interest to another party, but it's not home ownership. It's vacation home ownership.

We don't recommend time-shares, because they can be overpriced and difficult to resell. But if you're sure that you want to vacation in the same place every year, a time-share can buy you a stable place to stay.

EQUITY SHARING: THE WILD WEST AND "OVER THERE"

Don Donahue is a real estate broker in fashionable Marin County, California, just north of San Francisco, where home prices are so high that equity sharing has become the new wave. He tells many amusing stories of people who have succeeded in buying an equity share, but some have no ending. They are happy stories as far as they go, but it remains to be seen what their final outcomes may be.

Mary Jane and Bill Monette, however, did great. They bought a 50 percent share in a lovely, four-bedroom, two-and-a-half-bath Spanish style house in the upscale community of San Rafael. The house was priced at $350,000 (in 1990), but the Monettes paid literally no down payment and required no credit, which was just as well since Bill had declared bankruptcy when his small software development company in Alameda went belly-up a year earlier.

They did pay all the costs of closing the deal and the entire agent's commission, so it cost them well over

$20,000 to get into the house, and they took on the $3,000-a-month mortgage payment. Mary Jane's excellent job as a public relations coordinator for a group of Napa wineries earned enough to keep up the payments, but they quickly became house rich and cash poor. Gone were the weekend flights to Utah for skiing. Bill and Mary Jane learned to stay home and play Monopoly and have their friends over for cheese, crackers, and (complimentary) Napa wine.

Nonetheless, they lived in grand style in what had been the home of a top San Francisco import-car dealer. They had a redwood sauna, small lap pool, distant view of the lights twinkling over the bay and the great span of the Golden Gate Bridge. They had Persian rugs and three fireplaces and two Airedale terriers. And Bill launched a new business in personalized greeting cards, installing computer-run machines in chain drugstores and supermarkets that allowed customers to create their own sentiments on a printed card.

The only hitch was their five-year deadline to sell the house. After the first two and a half years passed, they became increasingly anxious. That is, under the agreement they struck with the sellers, they had five years in which to enjoy the house, after which they either had to buy out the original owners' half interest or sell the house and split the proceeds 50/50 . . . which turned out to be no problem, because the $350,000 house went for $585,000 in 1995 (and is probably worth at least twice that in 2003).

As for the sellers, they were delighted when the Monettes purchased the equity share, because they'd simply exhausted their resources keeping up with the high mortgage payment, staggering utilities, and hidden costs of maintaining such a nice home. The place just about demanded a gardener and housekeeper, unless you were home all day with nothing to do but housework. The sellers were happily installed in a relatively less expensive apartment in Berkeley, vastly relieved to be free of the mortgage burden and other costs of the home.

"That's the funny thing about some of these equity-sharing deals," says agent Don. "You can get into a really fantastic house for nothing down or with no credit, because the sellers just plain flat out can't afford to keep up their payments and they can't find a regular buyer for some reason. Some of these properties are blue ribbon, the best. And they'll let anybody in there who can cover their butts on that mortgage payment."

Anybody? Yes, anybody with money. Credit doesn't matter.

Another Berkeley-based homeowner looking for an equity-share partner in 2003 is Karen Sharpe, and author Ray Mungo is interested. You might be, too. Although she owns three houses in Berkeley, Karen currently lives in Paris, France, where she'd like to quit renting and purchase a home. But Karen is daunted by the high real estate prices in France aggravated by the fall of the U.S. dollar against the euro in the wake of the invasion of Iraq. Ray has long had a dream of owning a tiny studio apartment in Paris for his part-time use as a place to write, and otherwise to rent out to American teachers, writers, and tourists on a casual basis.

Karen is working on a deal that includes a two-story apartment on the top floors of a five hundred-year-old

building in the 4th arrondissement, close to the Louvre
and within walking distance of the Seine. With some
reconstruction, the large apartment can easily be made
into two separate units—a generous one bedroom with
sitting room for Karen and her dog, Moki, and a studio
upstairs for Ray and his tenants. Each unit would have
its own kitchen and bath.

Under French law, there is no way to break up the
ownership of this property into two separate legal enti-
ties. So the apartment will remain one piece of real estate, with Karen and her equity partner (Ray or
someone else) entering into a contract specifying each
person's share of the square meters and monthly costs.
Karen, with her three rental houses in Berkeley, has excellent credit and no difficulty obtaining a mortgage—
and French mortgages operate pretty much the same as
American ones do. There is no legal impediment to
U.S. citizens owning property in France, and many do.
There's even a tax advantage, as the IRS allows you to
deduct the mortgage interest you pay on a second
home, no matter where in the world it is. So with
Karen's terrific credit and Ray's (or someone else's)
money to make it affordable, this deal could be a fait
accompli by the time you read this. Anyone for cham-
pagne?

PROS AND CONS OF SHARING EQUITY

There's no question that equity sharing can be a terrific
device for the renter lacking good credit who wants to
get into home ownership. There are pitfalls and dan-
gers, however, and you can't be too careful in making

sure that all the details are handled in a legal and proper fashion that protects your interests.

The contract between you and the seller, entering into an equity-sharing agreement or partnership, should be checked by an attorney experienced in real estate matters. In most real estate transfers, a lawyer's services are not required, but in this case we strongly urge you to get professional advice before putting your money on the line.

Owning property (even if it's only a half interest) tends to improve your credit rating, so it's possible if you share equity that you may see your credit rating rise. This is a tendency, not a rule. If you have judgments against you or old bills left unpaid, they will remain on your credit report and no amount of home ownership will make them disappear.

In any sharing arrangement that is based on the idea that you will sell the home in a specific number of years and split the proceeds, you are running a calculated risk. What if some unforeseeable change occurs that makes the house impossible to sell? What if the house actually goes down in value over the time elapsed? What if a natural disaster like an earthquake levels the place and the insurance doesn't cover it? It could happen.

Take a calculated risk, but not a foolish one. Make sure that legal title is correctly transferred (vested) into your name, and duly recorded in your county recorder's office. Study the values and comparable prices of other houses in the neighborhood, and inquire into the trend of real estate prices in the vicinity. Have prices been stagnant, gone up, or gone down?

More than that, look into the greater external factors

that might affect the future value of the home. Is there a major highway or other large construction project planned nearby? Is your view obstructable should someone put up a high building across the street? What is the quality of the school district, and how healthy is the local employment market? These are gravely important considerations when you are, in effect, betting that you can sell the house for a profit in x years' time. Even the nicest house could be difficult to sell if there are no jobs in town.

Most important, be sure you know the person(s) with whom you are planning to enter into this partnership. We are basically bullish about equity sharing; it's a good idea in some circumstances, but we've also heard horror stories from people who bought real estate with a partner and later quarreled with that partner. In the worst of worlds, such squabbles can lead you into a courtroom, suing or being sued for partition (forcing the sale of the house against one party's wishes), paying lawyers, and being miserable and anxious.

A partition judgment usually happens when one partner wants his or her cash out of the property but the other partner can't afford to buy them out. The place is sold, and the money divided.

Find out if the equity-sharing partner has any history of litigation. If the seller has shared equity with others, phone those people and ask them if they are happy with the arrangement. Inquire into the reputation and financial stability of anyone with whom you are considering sharing property.

Home ownership is a highly emotional matter for many people, and for most of us the home is our single greatest investment. If you do have a falling out with your equity partner, it can be a devastating and bitter experience. So go forth bravely, but cautiously and sensibly.

EQUITY SHARING AND PARENTS

Parents of adult children are ideal candidates for equity sharing, and often this is a way they can help their kids acquire a home, by using their good credit for the mortgage and their savings for the down payment. Typically, the adult children live in the house and make the mortgage payments. In time, they can sell the house and split the profits, or buy out their parents' share, or perhaps inherit the parents' interest.

Even easier, in cases of complete familial trust, the parents can buy the property together with the children as joint tenants with right of survival. That way, should the parents die, the children are automatically the sole owners without going through probate court, or paying any taxes based on the increased value of the property. Joint tenancy is joint ownership, pure and simple, and "right of survival" means the last one standing holds the bag.

Reggie and Pearl Harper did exactly that with their three children. As each kid reached the age of twenty-one, they bought a condo in joint tenancy with that child, and allowed the child to live in it. The home ownership instantly conferred good credit on the young person, and in time all three moved on to purchase single-family homes. The Harpers held on to the condos and made them into rentals. Now in their eighties,

Reggie and Pearl are literally millionaires after starting with nothing and working hard all their lives. When they die, their kids will continue to own the condos and collect the rents, or perhaps allow their own children to move in!

EQUITY SHARING AND TAXES

The investor (parent, friend, or business associate) who puts up the down payment but does not live in the house can still get some hefty tax benefits from the equity-sharing arrangement. The way it's done is that the nonresident partner officially rents his or her half of the house to the resident partner.

The rent is precisely equal to the nonresident's half of the mortgage payment plus taxes and insurance. That way, the nonresident can also claim depreciation deductions, under IRS Schedule E. Depreciation is an income tax deduction available to landlords to compensate for general decline and upkeep expenses of a home. There is a limit to the deduction based on the landlord's income. Consult your tax advisor for the latest changes in IRS rules, but be sure to point out to your parents or cobuyer that these tax advantages are available.

EQUITY SHARING AND TROUBLE

There is one significant danger for the nonresident investor, and that is the difficulty in getting rid of a resident investor if that person simply stops paying the mortgage or their agreed share. It's not as easy to evict a co-owner as it is a tenant. And if you, the resident co-owner lacking credit, should happen to declare bankruptcy, your creditors can attack your half interest in the property, which could be a real nightmare to the nonresident investor.

These are thorny, if unlikely, problems that reinforce our advice that you should be very careful to maintain an excellent rapport with your equity partner. Even parents and children can fight over property and never speak to each other again.

Don't enter into an equity share unless you really trust your partner, and don't do it without a legal written contract, as required by IRS Code 280A.

After all those scary warnings, however, we still think equity sharing is a perfect vehicle for some people without credit to get into home ownership.

EIGHT

Foreclosure to You

What a racket it is. In 2004, the U.S. is experiencing record-high rates of both foreclosure on homes and personal bankruptcy. These rates of foreclosure and default on real estate loans surpass even the Great Depression. The sad truth is that three million jobs were lost, mostly in manufacturing, between the 2000 presidential election and the end of 2003, and a lot of honest people are getting to the point where they can't keep up payments as they agreed to, so in the end they may lose their property in foreclosure.

Or, if they are lucky, they may sell the property just in the nick of time before foreclosure, thus preserving their credit rating. And you, the buyer lacking credit, could well be the new owner of such a property.

Just as in the Depression, professional investors who have some cash on hand and/or good credit can now swoop in and buy those foreclosed or distressed properties at bargain-basement rates. These individuals attend the foreclosure auctions with their pockets literally full of cash (or cashier's checks) and pick up good houses for a fraction of their former value.

This practice has given rise to a new kind of no-credit home purchase which we call "foreclosure to you." The professional buys the house, then turns around and sells it as quickly as possible to the buyer with inadequate credit, at a profit. The investor finances the purchase so you don't have to qualify at a bank or mortgage company. In some cases, you don't need a down payment, just closing costs.

But you may pay a higher price, and you should be extra careful whom you are dealing with. It's only reasonable to assume that people who make a specialty of buying houses in foreclosure auctions or from desperate sellers on the eve of foreclosure will not hesitate to foreclose on *you* if your payments fall behind.

Nonetheless, we encourage you to look into these deals, because they can provide a way for you to stop paying rent and get into home ownership without credit, and as long as you can meet the terms and have safe, legal title, something like this could be just what you need.

Mike F. and Steve P. are examples of professional investors who sell houses in this fashion in Phoenix, Arizona. Both of them run newspaper ads saying, "I sell houses. No qualifying. I'll finance. Phone xxx-xxxx." They don't actually have any listings. They take calls from prospective home buyers like yourself, talk to you about what kind of house you're looking for, which neighborhoods you're interested in, and how much you can afford. Then, they go out and try to find a house for you. Mike even says, "Find a house you like, and I'll buy it for you!"

They look for houses that are either in foreclosure proceedings or already foreclosed upon. The court is required to publish the addresses of property scheduled for foreclosure, and those lists are public knowledge. You can go to your county clerk's office and ask for a copy of the most recent list of homes scheduled for foreclosure court. Then you can drive around and inspect homes that are on the "endangered list." Up to the moment the foreclosure happens, you can still buy the house directly from the owner. Sometimes this is called "a race to the record," because many home purchases take place mere hours or minutes before the foreclosure is about to happen.

Once the foreclosure is final, however, the house may be put up for auction in the court, and anyone can bid on it. The only hitch is that the court will demand cash for the property. In other words, an investor with good credit can pick up a distressed property for a down payment and get a mortgage one way or another, but a foreclosed property sold at auction requires cash on the barrel.

In either case, however, the investor can turn around and sell the house to you, even if you have no credit.

Mike F. has adopted a new concept in financing—the forty-year home mortgage at a slightly-above-average interest rate. He buys the home for you, the home you've agreed in advance that you want, then sells it to you on a wraparound for a down payment and monthly mortgage payments that guarantee him a good profit. The forty-year mortgage has a due-on-sale clause, meaning that you have to cash Mike out if you sell the place. Typically, he says, people sell within seven years. Few people would pay off a mortgage over forty years, but if they did, they'd have paid for the house many times over. The profit is in the interest, of course.

Mike's a nice enough guy, but he's not in the business of being charitable to people who fall behind in their payments. You could say he fairly circles overhead like a vulture, waiting for his moment. "Look, I feel sorry for these people," he says, "but I didn't create their problems." And he didn't create your problems with credit, nor will he give you any kind of grace if you should lose your job or your health.

You can work at finding houses that are just about to be foreclosed on and approach the owners yourself. It's called buying property "subject to" the existing mortgage, which is not the same thing as assuming the existing mortgage because, although you take over the payments and gain full legal title to the house, the former owner remains liable for the loan if you should default.

It works like this: by some means or other, usually through advertising in small venues like free weekly newspapers, you try to find an owner who is behind on his or her payments and facing the humiliation and loss of imminent foreclosure. You have enough cash on hand to pay all that person's back payments, bring the mortgage up to date, and take over the payments. In some cases the lender may not even be aware that the property has changed hands, but in any case as long as the payments are being made on time, the lender is unlikely to pursue a due-on-sale clause because the original owner is still responsible for the debt and the interest rate may well be higher than the current interest rates.

The desperate kind of owner who will sell his house subject to the existing mortgage gets only one thing out of it—relief. Relief from the payments, and relief from the fear of destroying his or her credit rating. But this seller may worry a great deal about continuing to be liable for the mortgage, so one way to allay his fears is to build in a time limit after which you agree to pay off the seller's loan, such as a five or seven year balloon payment.

FORECLOSURE SCAM ARTISTS

Mike at least appears to be completely honest and legal. He's been in the business for many years, answers his own phone, and has great references. Not everyone in the foreclosure game is necessarily above board, however. Buyer beware this kind of scam, which we have observed being practiced up and down the West Coast:

The ad in the paper says, "Why pay rent? We buy foreclosure houses at auction and sell to you for nothing down, no credit required." You call and get a tape-recorded message that goes on for several minutes with a pitch that's just too good to be true. "Enroll in our program and we'll show you how to get rich in seven to eight years. We provide you with listings for over five hundred foreclosure houses a month. Pick out the house you want, we'll buy it for you at auction and sell it to you for nothing down, with no qualifying, no credit. But since you are paying nothing up front, the only thing we ask you to pay is the closing costs, typically about $1,500. You don't need a job or credit references, but you must have $1,500 for the closing costs. Sound easy? It is! Leave us your name and phone number so we can invite you to our next free seminar, where we explain how our system works."

There are variations on this theme, but these outfits always have a clever-sounding name around the idea of quitting paying rent. "Landlord Busters," "Foreclosure Kings," "Rent No More." You can never reach a live individual on the phone; they must call you back. And they won't give you the details until you come to their "free informative seminar."

The catch, every time, is that they want you to pay the $1,500 (or $1,250, or $2,000) "closing costs" in advance. This is your fee for "enrolling" in their "program." And they assure you that the full amount will be applied to your closing costs when they buy you that foreclosure home at some time in the future. They are careful to state that they will *bid* on the house for you, but there is no guarantee their bid will be accepted.

We have no evidence that such schemes are illegal or dishonest, but despite much investigation we've yet to find a single person who actually bought a house using these programs. Our advice is *don't* ever hand over a fee for closing costs or anything else on a house you haven't bought or seen yet. And remember when they tell you about the five hundred listings a month that foreclosure notices are public record. You can get the same lists without paying a cent. It's very easy for these fast-talking artists to string you along for months, telling you that the house you wanted was outbid. And it's easy for them to pack up and leave town after they've gotten enough people to "enroll" in their "program" and pay up front.

This is not just paranoia. Alas, there are crooks in

the real estate business, as if you didn't know. Beware of anyone who is pushing "exclusive listings" that you have to pay for, whether for rentals, foreclosure sales, or any other kind of real estate. No honest agent or broker charges money to look at listings. Some of these scam artists go from town to town, changing their names and the names of their businesses. These outfits can look completely legitimate, with nice furniture, well-dressed sales people, seminars held in major hotels. Beware if the company is so new that it's not listed in the phone book. Insist on references. Demand proof. Ask to meet in person at least three people who have bought a house through that agency, and ask to meet them in their houses. Most of all, don't pay in advance for anything until you are making a legitimate purchase offer on a specific house with an established escrow holder.

Having issued that warning, however, we still think foreclosure houses can be a wonderful opportunity to get a home without qualifying for credit.

MORE FORECLOSURE WARNINGS

The foreclosure auction can be a frustrating experience. They are often postponed or canceled at the last minute, and you can do quite a lot of running around with little to show for it. Also, things can happen so fast at an auction that the property you want is gone before you have a chance to make a bid. There even are cases of people who mistakenly bid on the wrong house, and wind up owning something they didn't want.

If you're even considering buying a foreclosed house, you owe it to yourself to attend a few of these auctions and quietly observe what goes on. It's another case of the rich getting richer. If you happen to have the cash on hand, you might be able to pick up real estate at 80 percent or less of its appraised value.

But don't fantasize that you can get a house for 50 percent of its value. The court will invariably establish a minimum bid, and that minimum price is a matter of public record. The foreclosure sharks attending the auction will carry a cashier's check already made out for the minimum amount, and an undetermined amount of cash to make up the difference if the successful bid is higher.

Another thing to consider with a foreclosed property is that it is always sold as is. That means if you later discover a serious flaw in the property, you have no recourse. You can inspect the property before you buy it, but sometimes even very serious problems are not obvious.

The final caveat here is emotional as well as financial. Ask yourself if you really want to buy a house that some other person has lost to foreclosure. It would be helpful to know exactly why the previous owner was unable (or unwilling) to make the payments. Was it a personal tragedy such as illness, death in the family, sudden loss of employment? Or was there something wrong with the house itself, or the neighborhood the house is in, which caused that homeowner to effectively give up?

Be very careful that somebody else's troubles don't become your own. It's not easy to get foreclosed upon.

Most banks and lenders will bend over backward to give the homeowner a chance to catch up on overdue payments. Long before foreclosure happens, the owner receives late-payment notices, warnings, letters, invitations to consult the credit counselor at the bank. Many mortgage lenders will accept a partial payment if the homeowner can't come up with the entire amount at one time. If nothing else, a homeowner can often sell the house (perhaps at a good profit) before being foreclosed upon. So why do people simply surrender their property?

It's an important question, and one you would be wise to ask before buying a foreclosed property. Some people become emotionally upset when they fall behind in their house payments, so they lock the door and turn off the phone and just do nothing, as if that will help solve the problem. While the slow, laborious process of foreclosure is lumbering along, they could be selling their home and at least retrieving their investment in it, but instead they wait until it's too late.

Buying such a distressed property, one that is scheduled for foreclosure but not yet foreclosed on, can be a terrific boon for the person with inadequate credit, however. The seller in a case like that is truly motivated, and may be happy to unload the home to anyone who can bring the payments up to date and take over the mortgage while giving him some cash for his equity. A lump sum of cash goes a long way toward healing the pain of losing the house.

The seller may even be able to finance the sale in a wraparound mortgage, where he continues to be responsible for his mortgage and you pay him directly. If you make a wraparound deal, however, be sure to insist on monthly proof that the previous owner has made his payment on the first mortgage—a photocopy of a canceled check, or receipt from the mortgage holder. Any homeowner who got within shouting distance of foreclosure may fall into arrears again, so beware. The person may be an innocent, honest homeowner with bad luck, or there may be a culprit such as alcohol or drugs involved, or just plain senility. We've seen helpless elderly people, unaware of the trouble they are in, lose their property in foreclosure even though they have money in the bank to pay the mortgage.

Remember that foreclosure is the most dire thing that can happen in real estate, and you need to be extra careful in buying foreclosed property. But with foreclosure rates reaching unprecedented levels in the early 2000s, there are plenty of deals out there.

FORECLOSURE LOOMS

We'd rather be in the business of dispensing happy tales, but foreclosure is never a happy event and there is usually a sad story behind it. Consider this ad: "Foreclosure looms. Hurry! Ocean view, 2 bdrm., 2 ba., possible assume FHA 7½. $115K. Hurry for best deal. By owner."

After years of buying houses and exposure to hundreds if not thousands of agents and sellers, it's easy to pick up the telltale signs of a desperate seller. The owner was eager to get rid of this property, to say the least.

"I'm being driven out of town," he admitted with disarming candor. "I haven't had any work for six months and can't find a job. They're on my case something bad."

"They" in this matter invariably meant the banks, the collection agents, the powers of financial responsibility and foreclosure.

The "ocean view" turned out to be a distant one, indeed. The house was in southeast San Diego, in the most gang-infested, graffiti-scarred, crack cocaine–plagued part of town, but located on a hill with a far-off view of the water. "The view would be better if I could ever get my neighbor to cut his tree," the seller said bitterly. Translation: bad neighborhood, drive-by shootings, unpleasant neighbor.

The assumable FHA loan at 7½ percent was for only $22,000. A second mortgage, also assumable without credit, was $68,000 and fixed at an amazing 17½ percent, with a large balloon due in only seven months' time. "I'm sure they'd be happy to let you assume the loan," the seller said. "They'll take anybody who will make the payment." The lender was a finance company that would gladly extend the term of the loan to any buyer willing to pay their sky-high interest rates.

Sorry to say, we expected this unfortunate seller to face the foreclosure rather than sell his home with the burden of that high-interest loan on top of the problems of his beleaguered neighborhood. His only hope lay in finding a buyer willing to pay 17½ percent interest at a time when qualified borrowers could get a mortgage under half of that, and even unqualified buyers could do a lot better. Or, he may have sold to a foreclosure specialist who turned it around and resold it quickly, before the balloon burst.

A FINAL WORD ON FORECLOSURE

Put simply, you need to be extra careful in dealing with foreclosed or about-to-be-foreclosed properties. We strongly advise you to consult an attorney to check any documents, or at the very least work with a professional real estate broker. Foreclosure deals are not for the faint of heart or the average home buyer. They are more complicated and can involve a tangled web of debts and claims (liens) against the property. Swim with these sharks at your own risk.

If you do find a foreclosure or other financially distressed house that you like, and it's available without credit, be absolutely certain that you receive clear, safe, and unclouded title at the close of escrow. A clouded title is one that is under dispute or subject to claims.

These deals are adventuresome, dangerous, and potentially very profitable. That's why you'll find a myriad, endless parade of books claiming to teach you how to "get rich quick" or "make big bucks" in foreclosure transactions. We are skeptical of such claims, but if you just want a place to live in and own, the possibilities are real.

NINE

Quitclaim

Nothing could be easier than quitclaiming as a method of acquiring property without credit. A quitclaim is simply a grant, whereby the owner of a house voluntarily signs over his or her interest to you, with or without payment. If you can find a person with good credit who is willing to buy a house with you, using his or her credit to qualify for the mortgage, then he or she can simply quitclaim the deed over to you, and voila, you become the sole owner despite having no credit.

There's no real catch to this except the obvious fact that a mortgage lender is not going to let the original borrower off the hook just because he quitclaims to you. If the mortgage is based entirely on that person's credit, then he or she will remain liable in case you fail to make your payments. The bank or lender can go after the quitclaimer.

That doesn't really matter as long as there is a great deal of trust between the two parties, the buyer without credit and the person who allows his credit to be used in this fashion—and as long as you make the payments on time. The lender will hold the original buyer responsible for the entire life of the mortgage, or until you sell the house and either pay off the mortgage or pass it on the new buyer.

This kind of arrangement is most likely to happen within a family, but no blood relationship is necessary, and some people are close enough friends to trust each other more than they trust their own relatives.

Doug Starr got his house in Joplin, Missouri, through a quitclaim from his grandfather. Doug was a twenty-five-year-old landscape gardener lacking enough credit for a mortgage, whereas his granddad had plenty of credit and a good reputation in the community, and the two got along well. In fact, grandfather and grandson bypassed Doug's parents, with whom neither of them got along.

They bought a two-story farmhouse together with the older man's credit qualifying for the mortgage, and with the understanding that Doug would take care of his grandfather and eventually receive full title to the house as part of his inheritance. They lived together for five years. Granddad had a stroke and later died, but not before he quitclaimed his share of the property to Doug for $5. (In some real estate deals and some states, there must be a monetary "consideration" to make a deal legal. It can be as little as $1, but you can't give away the property for nothing.) In the meantime, the house increased in value from about $40,000 to $60,000 five years later.

Doug was left with the deed to the house, the mortgage payment, and the full benefits of the gift. When he moved to Key West, Florida, to be a landscape artist for the rich, he rented out the farmhouse to his father, who had separated from his mother. If the arrangement seems a bit unusual, it's perfectly legal and it worked out fine for everyone involved.

Of course, the bank can no longer go after Doug's grandfather in case of any default, because he's dead. They could foreclose on Doug if he quit making payments, but he's always paid on time and that payment record alone has given him excellent credit. When he gets tired of Florida, he figures, he can eventually move back to Missouri and back into the house.

Andrew Malone didn't have such a gratifying experience with the duplex he bought with his mother in Manchester, New Hampshire. Everything was fine with Andrew and his wife and children living in one of the units, and his mother in the second, until the mother quitclaimed her interest to her daughter, Andrew's sister, Bridget.

That left the mother still liable for the credit, even though Andrew was (as always) paying the entire monthly mortgage amount, while his sister became his co-owner. Nothing went wrong with the arrangement until the mother died, Bridget married a teacher from Boston, and brother and sister quarreled. Although she'd never lived there and only recently acquired an interest in the duplex, Bridget and her new hubby demanded their share of the property in cash, which Andrew couldn't possibly raise. He was forced to sell the duplex to meet his sister's demands, and saw his own family displaced from a home they had occupied and paid the mortgage on for more than ten years.

Andrew and Bridget never spoke to each other after that. Andrew swore he'd never again buy property in conjunction with another person, not even a close relative. When, years later, Andrew finally bought another home, his credit was good enough to buy a single-family house. His story illustrates the hazards of a quitclaim arrangement, and the immense bitterness between family members that can result. It's not unusual for loved ones to part forever after fighting over real estate. Even when Andrew died and Bridget attended his funeral, Andrew's widow, Helene, refused to speak to her sister-in-law. These two ladies sat for three days on the opposite sides of the open casket containing Andrew's body. "I can't prevent her from being here," said Helene, "but after she took our house away, why should I have anything to do with her?"

And that's not even the worst-case scenario. Imagine the chagrin of landlady Sylvia Moss of Pueblo, Colorado, who liked her tenant Jim Babcock so much that she agreed to put up her substantial credit as a cosigner when Jim fell into a bargain deal on a great little bungalow. She quitclaimed her share over to Jim, as they had agreed in advance, but was dismayed when only six months later Jim couldn't keep up his mortgage payments and the bank went straight to Sylvia for relief. In fact, they gave up trying to collect from Jim even though he lived in the house, because he was out of work and Sylvia had more assets. Soon she was deluged with calls from collection agents. The friendship between former landlady and tenant became very strained.

Sylvia made a few payments to get Jim out of debt, and began nagging him to sell the bungalow if he couldn't pay his own mortgage. Because they were such good friends, Jim didn't want Sylvia to suffer, so he eventually sold the house and (you guessed it) went back to renting from Sylvia. The taste of home ownership had him addicted, however, and he started looking around for another house he could buy without credit but without Sylvia's partnership.

It is certainly possible that someone who quitclaims property to another person could wind up paying for the property for years to avoid besmirching their credit rating, while the smug creditless person sits in the house, legally owning something he hasn't paid for. It is possible, but we haven't found a single case of such a dire thing happening. Perhaps that's because the only person who would cosign for a mortgage and then quitclaim the property to someone lacking credit would be a very close relative or friend, someone in a relationship of absolute trust.

If you have such a person in your life, a relative or friend who is willing to trust you with a house mortgage, be glad! Don't hesitate to use that trust and love to feather your nest. You're one of the lucky ones.

It's worth adding that the person with good credit doesn't necessarily have to quitclaim the property to you, the buyer without credit. In some cases, people simply buy property together and hold it together, as an equity-sharing arrangement. One party has credit, the other doesn't. The banks don't care how bad your credit is as long as your partner's is excellent and that person is willing to take full responsibility in case you flake out and miss payments.

The quitclaim action can happen the day after you buy the house, or any number of years later. It's remarkably simple. The giver of the quitclaim signs a quitclaim form available at any stationery store, in front of a notary public witness, then files the form with the county recorder. It's not even necessary to inform the bank, which has no role to play and no power to prevent the transaction.

In the case of a parent and child buying together, you may simply gain the other person's equity as joint tenants with the right of survivorship following a death. More about inheritance and buying from the elderly and dying follows in the next chapter.

TEN

En Viager and Buying from the Old, Dying, and Dead

You can't take it with you, according to the eternal verity, and so one way or another people who die have to pass along their real estate to another person or entity. We don't mean to be facetious. Obtaining property from the elderly or deceased isn't limited to inheritance.

The French have a system called *en viager*, which allows a homeowner over the age of sixty-five to sell the home while retaining the right to live there the rest of his or her life. In the United States, we have the life estate grant, similar to *en viager* in that the property changes hands but the elderly person retains a lifetime right to occupancy.

Reverse mortgages, estate liquidation sales to settle **probate**, and emergency sales to pay estate taxes are other ways that people without credit can and do buy real estate from the old, terminally ill, or dead.

Let's examine the French *en viager* system for a moment. We don't conventionally sell real estate in this fashion in the United States, but there's absolutely no law against it, and with some modification the same plan would work perfectly well in any country.

First of all, the seller must be sixty-five or older and will get the right to remain in the house until death, so the buyer is taking a gamble on the health of the seller. The seller will sometimes feign a terrible illness, moaning and groaning and acting as if he or she is only steps away from the grave. Then, the moment the sale is legal and complete, a sudden vigor returns!

The buyer pays the old person a down payment on the house, called a "bouquet," and promises to pay a certain amount every month. When the seller dies, the buyer acquires the house, with no further obligations to the seller's estate. If the seller owned the place free and clear, the buyer gets the property with no further payments of any kind.

The bizarre part of this, from an American point of view, is that there is no fixed price for the house. It all depends on how long the elderly person lives. If the seller dies soon, the buyer gets a terrific bargain. On the other hand, if the seller hangs on to the age of 110, the buyer could possibly pay two or three times the value of the house!

Another thing: if the buyer misses even one monthly payment, every penny (or euro) he or she has paid into the house is forfeited. Talk about motivation for getting your check in the mail! Some would say this arrangement could even be motivation for murder.

Buying real estate *en viager* is illegal in neighboring Switzerland. Not here in the U.S., however.

Clearly, this system works best with a seller who has no children or heirs, and who owns the house free and clear, with the mortgage paid off.

Applying the same principle to this country, lenders came up with the concept of the reverse mortgage, which has become increasingly popular. Reverse mortgage finance companies will buy a home from an elderly person, pay that seller a monthly amount, and take title to the property when the person either dies or moves out. The only real difference between reverse mortgages and *en viager* is that a definite price is established on the house. When the old person dies, the reverse mortgage company still must pay off the difference owed on the house to the seller's heirs or estate. The seller is guaranteed a monthly check for life, however, so it's possible the company could pay more than the house is worth if the owner lives a long time. These companies work from insurance statistics with fairly reliable predictions of how long a person will live. The amount they pay every month depends on how old the seller or sellers are, and how much the house is deemed to be worth.

There's no reason why an individual buyer couldn't essentially issue a reverse mortgage to an elderly seller. Many older people are house rich but cash poor. They've worked hard all their lives, paid off a mortgage, and watched their house increase in value perhaps twenty or thirty times over. They're sitting on a gold mine but living on chicken feed. A reverse mortgage allows them to get extra money every month and substantially improve the quality of their lives, without having to leave their home. And that can be a great deal for both the pensioner and the struggling buyer without credit, because the vast majority of older homeowners want nothing more than to stay in their homes for life, comfortable and safe with an income that protects their dignity.

LIFE ESTATE GRANTS

Many older homeowners essentially give their property to their children, but retain a lifetime use of the place. This is a simple life estate grant, and the purpose is to avoid probate. When the parent dies, the inheriting child is already the legal owner of the house and doesn't need to pay taxes or get involved in complicated procedures for taking title.

The personal reverse mortgage we suggested earlier is nothing more than a life estate grant in which you as the buyer are paying for the property rather than getting it for nothing.

By the way, a life estate grant always includes a clause that requires the homeowner to keep the property in good repair and pay the taxes. If your elderly parent or seller gets Alzheimer's disease or just becomes cranky and uncooperative and lets the house go to shambles, you as holder of the life estate grant have a legal right to enter the premises, make the repairs, and otherwise protect your property, even though you can't take possession until the older person passes on.

If you have a close friend who is getting along in years, has no children or heirs, and owns a home outright, you're only a breath away from making a deal that will eventually get you a home without needing credit. There are also times when people make an agreement to take care of an older person, be a nurse and companion, in exchange for eventually inheriting the property. All such arrangements, reverse mortgages and life estate grants, must be in writing and legally binding. This is one area in which we strongly recommend you employ a competent attorney to draw up the papers.

There are many unfortunate things that can happen to an elderly homeowner, of course. What if the person's health deteriorates so much that he or she must go into a nursing home? With most life estate grants, the seller retains a right to the home even in that circumstance. The reasoning here is that perhaps health will improve, and the elderly person should have the right to go back to his or her home. It's a very humane arrangement, all things considered, and it need not be exploitative.

Everybody knows some senior citizen who lives alone in an older home. By purchasing a home from an elderly person, you could be that person's angel and best friend.

BUYING FROM THE DEPARTED

Not to be morbid, but if you can buy a house from a terminally ill or elderly person, you can certainly also buy one from a deceased person. All kinds of things can happen to their real property when people die, even if there are heirs. Look for estate liquidation sales (probate) and emergency sales to pay estate taxes, and you may find property that you can buy without credit simply because the sellers have an urgent need to get rid of it.

A classic example is a house author Ray Mungo bought from the estate of Minnie Skinner in Seattle. She had died in the house after going blind there, stringing nylon stocking ropes all over the place at waist level to guide her through the rooms. The only heir was a distant nephew who had no use for the house and wanted only to sell it as soon as possible to settle Minnie's probate, taxes, and estate. The nephew hired a lawyer who sold the house to Ray with no credit check, for nothing down but the promise of a deferred down payment to be made in a year's time.

The place was a wreck but it had potential. It also had a small apartment attached in the rear, rented out to a young single woman who often had boyfriends over and loud beer parties on weekends. In a funky touch, Minnie and the tenant shared the same phone, which they passed back and forth through a hole in the wall separating their different living spaces. With the help of friends, in less than a year Ray had fixed the place up and sold it for a tidy profit—even before the down payment came due. The nephew got his cash out of it and Ray went on down the road, looking for the next deal.

So be sure to read the obits. Become a volunteer at the local senior citizens' center. Be an advocate for the elderly and you could buy yourself a great home without credit.

Of course, you cannot legally or ethically take advantage of an elderly person who is lacking in mental competence. We can't state this too emphatically. There are unscrupulous individuals who do just that, but their actions are reprehensible.

If the elderly person is declared mentally incompetent by a court or public authority, he or she doesn't have the legal right to transfer title to you or engage in a sale transaction. But even if the person has not been formally declared incompetent, if you take advantage of someone who's senile or incapable of handling his or her own affairs, that person's heirs or the district attorney can later sue you to retrieve the property, which would be considered stolen.

In an ideal situation, the elderly seller will have some professional advice or an advocate or representative not related or obligated to you, the buyer. And in all cases, your legal papers and transfers must be proper and airtight.

You cannot "take" property from the elderly but you can buy it without credit under the right circumstances to benefit the older person and yourself as well.

ELEVEN

The Unwanted, the Desperate, and the Ugly

As the chapter title suggests, you have a far better chance of buying a house without credit if the house itself is what we politely term "property in trouble." That doesn't mean it isn't a good house, worth owning, but only that for one reason or another it's difficult to sell. Therefore, the owner may be willing to sell it to an unqualified buyer, or indeed any buyer.

There are a thousand good reasons why somebody might need to sell a house, reasons that don't affect the value of the house itself. Divorce, death, bankruptcy, job transfer, illness, or imprisonment are all examples of bad things that can happen to good people, who then *must* sell their home, perhaps urgently.

But this chapter looks at the house itself and pinpoints areas in which the problems with the real estate may make it possible for you to buy without credit. Just be sure that whatever is wrong with the house is something you can fix, tolerate, live with, or otherwise accept!

1. Location, location, location. This is the oldest axiom in real estate. The location of the home is probably more important than the home itself, because you can't change where it is no matter how much you might improve the house. And a bad, or less than desirable, location can make a house very difficult to sell. A few examples:

- **Directly in front of or next to a school.** Even parents with school-age children don't necessarily want to live near a school. Kids are loud, and nothing is louder than hundreds of them en masse, arriving in the morning and leaving in the afternoon and hanging around the playground or schoolyard. In some inner cities, schools can also attract drug dealers, gangs, petty violence, vandalism, and theft. Oddly enough, however, not everybody hates living near a school. We find that some people enjoy living near an elementary school simply because they absolutely love small children.

- **In a dangerous, crime-infested neighborhood.** How much do you value your safety? Few things will reduce the value of a home more than a vicinity known for its crime rate. If you can put up with security locks on your door, vandalism of your car, constant vigilance, and apprehension, you can sometimes get a wonderful house without credit that would cost double in a better neighborhood. Banks are not legally allowed to "red-line" certain neighborhoods, that is, exclude them from loans, but be realistic. A mortgage lender will be reluctant to invest in a bad location. That reality might force the seller to offer financing without qualifying credit. Also, be optimistic. Many a bad neighborhood has been improved and rehabilitated under the right circumstances. Famously, the so-called yuppies of the 1990s renovated some of the worst slums around Boston so that a "three-decker" house (a three-story, boxlike, humble multifamily structure) became a "Queen Anne."

- **In an area with a depressed economy and high unemployment.** Seattle in the 1970s, Dallas in the 1980s, Phoenix in the 1990s, Detroit in the 2000s are examples of cities where slumping local economies drove down the prices of homes. When there are few jobs available in a town, you'll find vacant homes abandoned by owners who were forced to move on, looking for work. If you're one of the lucky people with a stable job, or you're self-employed, a weak economy can actually help you buy without credit. If the economy rebounds and new jobs open, your house may increase tremendously in value.

- **At a great distance from civilization.** Sometimes rural property is a lot cheaper and easier to buy than convenient, urban real estate, unless the rural area happens to be a prosperous resort. If you're willing to live way out in the middle of nowhere, commuting a long way to your job or working from home, you'll get a lot more house for less money. Some farming communities in the Midwest have become virtual ghost towns. And some distant places actually get developed and transformed—Henderson, Nevada, not far from Las Vegas, is one of the fastest-growing communities in the nation but was an empty piece of desert only a few years ago.

- **In a place with bad weather.** You can't really overstate the importance of climate to real estate values. If the house is located in a town that gets brutally hot (like certain parts of Florida and the California desert) or unbearably cold (northern Michigan, North Dakota) or is subject to windstorms, tornados, floods, any kind of severe weather, you might find a homeowner who will do anything to move on. Make sure the weather is something you're willing to tolerate! There are rare individuals who claim to thrive on 120-degree heat or 30-below-zero cold. Of course, extreme weather will drive up your utility bills for heating or air-conditioning, as well.

- **In a noisy neighborhood.** Most of us don't want to live in a place that's roaring with noise. Just recently, a beautiful Victorian home in San Diego went for $11,000 down and $1,000 a month with no qualifying credit. The house was in excellent condition, with a large yard, but it was located right next door to a twenty-four-hour gas station on a busy, congested intersection with four lanes of incessant traffic. Not a peaceful location, but the proud new owners plan to construct a brick wall around the property borders.

- **Near an airport or along a freeway or major road.** Houses can be advertised as "convenient to the airport," which is just about the worst thing a house can be! Before buying a home under a flight path or in the vicinity of an airfield, be sure to go there and test the decibel level of airplane noise at all times of day or night. The same goes for houses located beside a freeway, interstate highway, or other major road. Studies have shown that folks who live in proximity to a freeway can suffer greatly from insomnia, depression, and headaches, and there's also some concern for environmental pollution.

- **In an area scheduled for major construction.** Ask the agent and the seller and double-check if you have any suspicion that a major highway or any big construction project is scheduled in the neighborhood. Sometimes, good houses are virtually given away because the neighborhood is about to become intolerable. And the seller is not necessarily obliged by law to disclose it, so beware. Author Robert Yamaguchi has neighbors in Signal Hill, California, who bought a lovely condo with a great view, completely unaware that a huge housing development was planned across the street. After two years of migraine-inducing, pounding construction work, their view is gone and every window of their condo looks directly into the new houses. They threatened to sue the sellers for not disclosing this scheduled development but got no relief.

- **With objectionable neighbors.** You'd better believe that the neighbors affect the value and salability of a home, and it's wise to find out anything you can about them before you buy. If the house next door looks seedy, with all kinds of debris and junk strewn around the yard, consider what kinds of people live there. If they keep a vicious dog on a chain, barking all night, how are you going to get your sleep? If the couple get drunk and scream at each other every Friday night, are you going to call the police and risk their enmity, or just put up with the noise? More than just the immediate next-door neighbors, consider the demographics of the entire community. We've seen some wonderful homes that were hard to sell because of the neighbors, but somebody else's bad relationships don't necessarily carry over to you.

These are a few location problems. No doubt you can imagine others. Let's go on to other problems of the desperate, the unwanted, and the ugly.

2. The price. Sometimes a house is difficult to sell simply because the owner is asking too much for it and refuses to come down on the price. If you're willing to pay a bit more, you might be able to swing a deal without credit. All real estate agents will give you comparables, prices that nearby homes with similar features sold for within the preceding six months. A bank may refuse to finance a mortgage for more than 80 percent of its appraised value. But a smart seller can sometimes get a higher price if he or she is willing to offer creative financing without credit approval. The interest rate on the loan may be higher, too. And you may be quite willing to pay a higher amount for the convenience of such financing.

3.   The utilities. If the house has very high utility bills, it may be harder to sell and therefore available without credit. Check into this carefully. Before buying any home, ask to see the last three to six months' utility bills. A house that costs a fortune to heat in the winter or cool in the summer can really tear into your budget. Remember, however, that some utility bill problems can be corrected. The house may need to be reinsulated, rewired, or changed over to another form of heat. You might be able to cut the water bill in half if you install slow-flow faucets and drip irrigation and the like. If you do find high utility costs, by all means use that as an argument to lower the price of the home or talk the owner into easier credit terms.

4.   The owner has moved. When a house is vacant and the seller has moved, he is doubly motivated to sell because he's probably paying his old mortgage as well as the costs of his new place to live. That can become a tremendous burden, so that the seller becomes desperate for someone, anyone, to move into the house and relieve him of the payments. Nothing is worse for a house than sitting empty, because of the risk of vandalism as well as general, slow disintegration. But nothing is better for a buyer lacking credit than an empty house that's been on the market for six months or more! Such a house is an ideal candidate for owner financing, lease option, equity sharing, or even adverse possession.

Conventional real estate thinking is that the best way to sell a house is when it's furnished, occupied, and looks its best. Our advice is to hunt for exactly the opposite: a house that's empty and looks its worst. It's helpful to know exactly why the owner moved, but there's no guarantee he'll tell you the truth. There are endless legitimate reasons for moving that don't diminish the value of the house, however. It may also be possible for you to do a more thorough investigation of the condition of the property simply because it's empty.

Find a house that's been empty for six months, and you're very likely to find a motivated seller. Check the date of the initial real estate listing.

5.   The property is in bad condition. This is an obvious problem that could lead to your being able to buy a house without credit. Naturally, you have to decide for yourself just how bad a condition you're willing to accept. If the house has serious structural problems, such as a cracked foundation or a roof that is falling down, you'd be well advised to get guaranteed professional estimates on the cost of the repairs before making an offer to buy. Call in a reputable contractor, plumber, electrician, or whomever and ask them to give you a quote in writing and guarantee the price for at least six months. Don't take on a home-repair job that's way above your financial capability.

Some bad conditions are repairable with merely

cosmetic work, things like paint, wallpaper, floor tiles, carpets, and so forth. Other conditions can be wildly expensive to repair: faulty plumbing, termite rot, inadequate wiring, defective septic system, or a broken furnace, to name a few. If you're looking at a home that's in visibly bad shape, it's worth paying a professional home inspector for a thorough report.

Once you've determined precisely how much it will cost to bring the house into good repair, present those figures to the seller as an argument to reduce either the price or the terms. A house that can't pass inspection also may not qualify for a mortgage, so the seller may be forced to offer financing without qualifying credit.

6.   The floor plan is awkward. A bad floor plan can be a serious flaw in a house, and make it difficult to sell. It's hard to understand why some houses are built with ridiculously awkward interior arrangements, such as a bedroom that can be reached only by walking through a bathroom, or a laundry room inconveniently located in the cellar. Variations are endless. A good floor plan puts the living room in a dead-end location, so that you don't have to walk through it to get anywhere else in the house. A foyer or exterior porch is helpful for receiving guests and removing outer clothing in the winter. The kitchen should have a separate entrance from the outside, so kids and pets can go in and out without tracking dirt and debris all over the living room rug. A house has traffic patterns, with the heaviest use being in the kitchen and main bathroom. A lousy floor plan can be inconvenient, but it also might make the house undesirable enough to be available without credit.

7.   The assumable mortgage is problematical. Some older homes were mortgaged in the days of 17 percent interest and are stuck with a high payment. You would want to refinance the property, but that's not possible because you don't have the credit to qualify for a new loan. Sometimes the mortgage is an adjustable rate loan, leaving you with no assurance of how high the monthly payment could rise in inflationary times.

8.   The builder went bankrupt, or disappeared. This problem relates to newer homes thrown up by incompetent or corrupt builders and contractors who later go out of business or just vanish. It's a shocking national scandal. You've heard people say, "They just don't build houses like they used to," but that's not necessarily true. Some new homes are well constructed of sturdy materials. But some homes are just plain poorly made, and start falling apart even while they are relatively young. Watch out for small things like doors that don't close snugly, dampness on the basement floor, or cracks in the plaster. If you're looking at a home in a development of newer houses, by all means canvass the neighbors and ask them if they've had any problems with poor construction.

9.   The house has a defect that makes it unbankable. This final flaw in our list will vary from state to state and bank to bank. Certain specific defects in a house will effectively prohibit a bank from issuing a mortgage, thus forcing the seller to provide alternative financing. In some places, the banks will not mortgage a house that lacks a foundation, even though you can live quite comfortably in a house without a foundation in the warmer parts of the Sunbelt states. Sometimes, the house is unbankable because it's had earthquake damage or sits too low in a floodplain and is subject to annual flooding, or has irreversible termite damage. The point here is simply that if you can tolerate or repair the defect, you can often buy such a house without credit. If you can't repair the defect, however, you also won't be able to sell the house through conventional bank financing at some later time.

So, dear home buyer, go out there and hang out with the desperate, the unwanted, and the ugly. Somebody else's problem could be your financial salvation and your dream home!

TWELVE

Go for It! New Techniques for the 21st Century

If you've read this far, you realize that there are many perfectly legitimate ways you can buy a home without needing any credit or bank approval. We've looked at assumable mortgages with no qualifying required; owner financing; lease options; 30 percent down-payment financing; adverse possession; equity sharing; foreclosure sales; quitclaims; buying from the elderly and deceased; and buying unwanted or distressed property.

Now let's really talk. And let's look at the new opportunities and techniques that have emerged in the information age and the housing market of the early 2000s.

This kind of house buying is not for the faint of heart.

Anybody with a large down payment in cash and a terrific credit rating can walk into a bank and get a mortgage, assuming the house itself is up to the lender's standards. But those of us lacking the down payment or the credit, or both, have to be a lot more creative, aggressive, faithful, determined, persevering, persuasive, open-minded, and willing to take a risk.

These qualities may in fact describe the essence of a person or persons who can go out and buy a home despite lacking credit.

Here are some important guidelines to remember:

- .Be realistic. Figure out what you really, absolutely can afford to pay every month and find a home that costs no more. You're not doing yourself any favors if you get into a home purchase that's over your head and will cause you to fall behind in the payments. Include all the hidden expenses like closing costs, taxes, insurance, utilities, and PMI, or private mortgage insurance, which is frequently added to a payment in cases where the mortgage is for more than 80 percent of the home value.

(There are several ways to get around PMI. One is called the 80-10-10 formula. You make a 10 percent down payment, the first mortgage is for 80 percent of the price, and the seller carries back a second mortgage of 10 percent. Another method is the 80-15-5, where the mortgage is 80 percent, there's a 15 percent home equity loan, and the down payment is 5 percent. But the best and easiest way to avoid PMI is to take over the seller's payments on an existing mortgage worth 80 percent or more of the value and either cash out the seller for the balance or pay him a second mortgage.)

Be realistic also about how much of a home you can get. Don't torture yourself longing for a swimming pool, a spiral staircase, or the ritziest neighborhood in town if you can't afford those things. It's just common sense that the nicer and more expensive the house is, the more a seller is going to worry about your credit. Remember that you can start with a smaller, less expensive home and build up your credit rating tremendously simply by paying your mortgage every month; every few years, with luck and work, you may be able to work up to a better house, until that mansion is eventually yours.

• **Be flexible.** This is very important. If the house you want isn't available without credit, don't mourn. Find another house. If the terms you offer don't work, or the seller is not convinced, write another offer, change the terms, try another route. If the real estate agent is an unimaginative, nay-saying, discouraging, "you-can't-possibly-afford-to-buy-a-house" type, find another agent. A flexible agent with some imagination could be your biggest asset.

The exact deal you seek may not be possible. You may have to beg your old Uncle Pete for a loan, or sell your recreational vehicle to raise the money for a down payment. You might have to rent out a spare bedroom to meet the mortgage. Maybe you need to find an equity share because you simply can't afford to own a whole house on your own. Try everything. Examine all possibilities.

• **Don't give up.** No advice we can give you is more important than this. Trying to buy a home without credit can be a discouraging process, and you could be turned down again and again. If you give up too easily, you'll just be a renter all your life.

Buying a house is a mental game as well as a physical purchase. Take the attitude that if you don't get the house, it was not the right house for you! Another, better house is waiting for you somewhere. The right house is the one that's easy for you to buy.

If you don't succeed, pick yourself up, dust yourself off, and go after something else.

You could hit it lucky and find your dream home on that first Sunday that you go out looking around. But that's unlikely and perhaps not even desirable. Most people have to shop around and see at least fifty houses before finding the right deal. If that takes months or even years, don't despair. Don't give up!

• **Be honest.** Don't waste your own and the agents' and sellers' time looking at houses you can't possibly get on no-credit terms. Tell everyone up front what your situation is, and what you need; how much, if anything, you can come up with as a down payment; how much you can pay every month; how bad your credit, if any, really is. Get to the bottom line and adhere to it. Tell the truth and you have nothing to fear. Lie and exaggerate and waffle, and you could get into serious trouble. If you are honest, you are going to look only at houses that have some real chance of selling to a buyer without credit.

• **Put it in writing.** There comes a time when all the talk amounts to nothing unless you make your offer in writing. Especially when you are trying to convince a seller to sell you the house without credit, you should be able to demonstrate in writing the profit that seller will receive. Most homeowners don't realize all the options.

The seller has established a sale price for the

house, and fantasizes about getting that much. "My house is worth $275,000 and my mortgage is only $120,000, so I'm going to get $155,000 when I sell the place!" is typical thinking. If, however, that same seller is willing to carry the paper (owner financing), he or she could actually receive double or triple the profit over a period of time! Prove it. Put it down on paper.

A savvy real estate agent will admit that if you write up an offer, *any* offer, you can never tell what will happen. Buyers have offered way below the asking price of a house, sure that their offer would be refused, only to have it accepted. One thing for sure is that you can't succeed if you don't make an offer in writing.

- **Get your free credit report.** The Fair and Accurate Credit Transactions Act of 2003 was signed into law December 4, 2003, and provides every American with the right to a free copy of his or her credit report once a year from the three major national credit rating firms: Equifax, Experian, and TransUnion. Previously, the major credit agencies were required to send you a free copy only if you'd been turned down for credit; otherwise they charged a service fee.

This new federal legislation also guarantees you the right to examine your **FICO** score, which is the basis on which lenders evaluate your qualifications for a mortgage. See below for instructions on how to improve that score! And the bill attempts to give law enforcement more tools with which to thwart perpetrators of identity theft, who wreck innocent victims' credit scores by fraudulent means.

The reason we urge you to exercise your right to order your credit report once a year is that you may find errors on that report, things that you can have changed which may improve your standing. Helpful real estate agents and brokers may be happy to assist you in documenting mistakes and correcting black marks on your name. It's quite common for old bills that you've already paid to still be showing up on your credit report! The IRS itself is notorious for failing to remove liens that have been fully paid off. It could be that your credit is not as bad as you think it is, or at any rate could be ameliorated. Even if it's absolutely terrible, it won't hurt you to know exactly what debts are being held against you and dragging your FICO score down. Remember that debts more than seven years old (except for debts to or guaranteed by the federal government) should be erased from your report under the statute of limitations laws. Check your own state's law on the statute of limitations.

And certainly any old bills, collection actions, court judgments, liens, late payments, or disputed charges that have since been cleared up or paid off and still sit on your credit report in error *must* be erased in order to improve your profile. Don't be afraid to complain, correct, insist on your right to an accurate report. Be proactive—ignorance is not bliss when it comes to your credit rap sheet. When you discover an error on your report, sit down and write a letter to the credit reporting agency explaining why the item is incorrect, and back it up with proof—for example, a photocopy of a receipt or canceled check showing you paid the bill, or a letter from the creditor affirming that you are in the clear. Keep a copy of any letters you send, and always mail them by certified mail so you'll have proof they were received. And keep after it—check your report periodically to see if the error has been corrected, and if it hasn't, write again. Remember it can sometimes take months to get these problems resolved, so be patient but vigilant. You can also telephone the credit reporting agencies and speak to a customer service operator, but in most cases you'll need to put your claim in writing anyway.

• **Be brave.** "Faint heart ne'er won fair lady," nor fine house. Buying a home can be scary and takes courage, because for most of us the home purchase is the single greatest investment we make in our lives. Of course you have to be careful, but you can't be timid or too conservative.

Our wise banking colleague, Lynne Ballew, refers to the whole of banking as "risk management," and home buying is similar. There's always a risk involved, and you can't win or even play the game without taking risks. Will the house appreciate in value, will it be worth more than what you paid for it in a few years' time, or will the market bubble finally burst? How about interest rates, will they go up or down? Will your business succeed? Will you get that promotion on your job? Take a chance, but not a foolish one. If you doubt that you know enough to take the risk, seek advice from someone whose real estate knowledge you respect. Don't be afraid, or you'll never get anywhere.

• **Do it now.** There's no time like the present. Real estate prices are notoriously cyclical; they can go up and down like a roller coaster, but historically if you look at the long run, adjusting for inflation, home values go up over time. There's no investment more fundamentally sound than a good, sturdy, well-cared-for roof over your head, and people will always value their homes above all else. You can worry about buying at the top of the market, only to find that there's no real top—prices may dip, but they will come back up again, and the ceiling just gets higher.

KNOW THE SCORE TO PLAY THE GAME

As mentioned above, your credit (if you have any at all) toward a mortgage is based on a scoring system devised by the Fair, Isaac & Co. credit reporting agency, and is called a FICO score. Scores run from the 300s to the 800s, rather like the college entrance exam SATs, and a FICO over 700 is generally considered excellent—it will get you the best terms, and lenders don't even ask you to document whether you have a job or any assets. If you score 660 or better, you can still get the lowest interest rates and best deals, but you have to show some evidence of your income, assets, and liabilities (whom you owe and how much). A score between 620 and 660 is marginal in the mortgage game; since you've got some kind of demerits showing that are pushing your score down, you can still qualify but not with just any mortgage lender.

And below 620, where countless millions of us dwell, is the subprime market. You don't qualify in the ordinary, conventional system, but—depending on how bad your credit really is—you just might be able to get an expensive loan reserved for risky borrowers with past delinquencies. (See below.) And you just might be able to improve your FICO score by even a few points and make a big difference in what's possible.

To find your own FICO score, go to the company's "My FICO" Web site at www.myfico.com and check yourself out. The company charges a fee for the information ($12.95 in 2004). There are numerous ways you can nudge your score upward and you can even use a professional mortgage broker who practices the art of rapid rescoring, submitting documents to clear up misinformation and improve your numbers. It's helpful to know what kinds of things affect your FICO score, such as:

- **The worst-case scenarios.** The most damaging things to your score are personal bankruptcy, collection agency activities, lawsuits resulting in a financial judgment against you, delinquency on a previous loan or, worst of all, foreclosure on a previous mortgage.

- **Late and still-owed payments.** Overdue payments and a history of being late or missing payments hurts your score.

• **Having only one credit card.** It's hard to see why this should bother a lender, but the score goes down if you have only one credit card and max it out, compared to borrowing the same amount of money but spreading it over two or three credit cards.

• **Having too many credit cards.** Yes, this can lower your score even if you have cards on which you owe nothing. Mortgage companies fear that you might run out and use all the credit available to you for things like home improvements, and thus get overburdened.

• **Applying for credit too often.** A record is kept of how many inquiries have been made to your credit report. Every time you fill out an application for credit, another inquiry is logged and your score suffers if there are "too many," but how much is too much depends on the individual.

• **NOT having certain types of debt.** It's helpful to have a car loan or any kind of installment loan, and in fact your score will be penalized if you don't have this kind of debt. One way around this is to put up a certificate of deposit (savings or CD) as collateral for a small bank loan, and pay that loan off in installments. Banks will issue the loan with the CD backing it up, since they have nothing to lose—you're essentially borrowing on your own money. As long as the interest rate is low, this is an easy way to create a higher score.

- **Paying things off.** It's been estimated that you could add as many as twenty points to your score by paying off one-third of your credit card or other debt.

- **Consolidating your debts.** This one is tricky because it either gains or loses you points depending on how you do it. Of course you want to bring your old debts together only if you're getting a better interest rate and a more affordable monthly payment. But at the same time, it's not good to saddle yourself with a gigantic debt to a single creditor, especially one that will take many years to pay off and also lower your score.

- **Checking for errors.** Misinformation is so common and can be so deadly to your FICO score that many people turn to the aforementioned mortgage brokers for help in rescoring. If you're looking for such a specialist, you can get a referral from the National Association of Mortgage Brokers online at www.namb.org.

SWIMMING IN THE SUBPRIME

But OK, no matter what you do to boost your FICO score, you may still be in the subprime market, and lucky to be even there. This market didn't even exist until recent years. Time was, you either qualified for a mortgage or you didn't. Now, you may not qualify for a regular mortgage, but there is very likely a lender, possibly located on the Internet and physically located outside the country, who will give you a mortgage at much higher interest rates, with all kinds of loan origination fees, extra points (charges based on a percentage), prepayment penalties (you're not allowed to pay early or pay down the interest), and personal mortgage insurance (PMI).

You may get fleeced. But at least you may be able to buy a home. The theory behind taking one of these so-called B-, C-, or D-level mortgages is that you have bad credit and, more than anything else, you need to build up some record and evidence of your ability to make a home payment on time. So, you play the subprime market game, make every payment right on time for a minimum of one year—two is better—then you apply to refinance the house at a preferable, more normal interest rate. In other words, prove yourself and improve yourself.

Some of these subprime lenders operate via e-mail and seem to reside only in cyberspace. You may be swamped with spam e-mails targeting people who want to buy a home but lack credit—a very large market of folks, so don't feel too bad. But don't be naïve, either. These people may indeed find you a mortgage lender, but there will be all kinds of upfront costs involved.

One actual recent e-mail reads: "Having trouble finding a mortgage because of bad credit? Have you been turned down before? Get free, no-obligation quotes from lenders who *understand your situation.* Get Free Quote—Click Here Now!" There's no indication of who exactly is sending this e-mail advertisement or who the lenders who "understand your situation" might be.

We don't wish to disclaim all online mortgage purchases as fraudulent or unsafe. In fact, the convenience of applying for credit online has brought an increasing percentage of home buyers and their agents to work over the Internet. And real estate agents will often accept a lower commission in exchange for the greater ease.

But it is still the agent, or broker, who is the key factor in most subprime mortgage trading. You, as the buyer lacking credit, are advised to find a broker who specializes in finding subprime loans for people in your situation rather than trying to do it yourself. An experienced broker may have literally hundreds of contacts in the lending field. He will jump on the computer and begin sending out trial balloons all over the place, and can get results and decisions back sometimes within minutes, decisions that in the regular world of banks might take weeks to arrive. Nonetheless, depending on how awful your credit really is, it might take months to find the right deal. As hard as it is to believe, however, some subprime brokers now make the claim that "almost" anyone can buy a house today, "almost" anyone can find a loan, regardless of their past credit history. It would be helpful to know just where the "almost" category ends and we pass into the "rarely" class.

Still, you have nothing to lose by exploring the subprime market as long as you don't fall victim to a fraud. First rule of thumb: never pay money in advance for the service of finding you a loan. Second, get some professional help from a knowledgeable agent or broker. And third, be aware that some subprime lenders deliberately refuse to report your mortgage payments to the major credit agencies, which has the effect of keeping your FICO score low—where they like it to be.

A final note to the wise: be wary of scam artists who promise to "fix" your credit report within thirty days for a fee, usually around $200. This blatantly phony service now crops up everywhere, on flyers nailed to phone poles, printed signs posted near the freeway on-ramp, small ads in weekly newspapers. It ought to be a crime. Nobody can doctor up your credit report and make all your problems vanish overnight, but people continue to be hoodwinked into paying for this bunk.

NO CREDIT HISTORY AT ALL—NO PROBLEM!

"Nontraditional" or "alternative" mortgage qualifying procedures have arrived on the scene, mostly in reaction to the presence of immigrants who come to the U.S. and want to buy a home but lack any credit history at all. These new procedures also apply to folks who for one reason or another simply don't use credit—sometimes for cultural or religious reasons—and thus don't have any scoreable records. These people pay their rent in cash, go to the phone company or electric company and pay utilities in person, or else the kind of personal bills they do pay are not the kind reported to FICO and the three major credit reporting agencies.

These programs eliminate the computer and score each applicant manually, a time-consuming process. They allow would-be buyers who have zero credit history to present alternative forms of proof of creditworthiness, like receipts showing they have paid their rent, utilities, and insurance premiums on time over a period up to several years. They liberalize the requirements for where a down payment can come from, so it's OK if a family pools its money or relatives loan money to each other to complete a purchase.

The target market here is the mortgage industry's effort to sell its product (home loans) to ethnic minorities, low-income people, recent arrivals to our shores as long as they have "resident alien" or legal immigrant status and a Social Security number. But you don't absolutely have to belong to those categories of people to get in on it. Huge lending giants including Freddie Mac, Fannie Mae, GMAC Mortgage, and First American Corp. are among the firms experimenting with these new, no-score-required mortgages. Ask a competent broker for assistance in locating these programs if you think you might be eligible.

GOOD NEWS IF YOU FIT THE BILL

Further good news for buyers struggling with credit problems comes in the form of a late 2003 decision by Sallie Mae, the giant student loan agency with seven million borrowers, to begin reporting student loan payments to the three major credit report agencies, which it previously did not do. If you're one of the many who have been able to keep up with your student loans despite having other credit problems, your Sallie Mae payments are going to have a beneficial effect on your FICO score, finally.

Also new on the scene are a staggering number of nontraditional lenders who never had anything to do with the mortgage business before—called "affinity" mortgage lenders. Instead of going to a bank or other lender, you apply for your mortgage financing from your college or university alumni association, your trade union (AFL-CIO has a program), your social organization or lodge, your employer, or even your church. All of these groups are getting into the act and, not surprisingly, buyers with inadequate credit elsewhere may find a more friendly reception with their own "affinity groups." Just as it's perceived to be easier to get a loan from a member-owner credit union than a commercial bank, you might get a mortgage from your union because you've got a pension fund built up, or from another group that you belong to which is likely to give you more benefit of the doubt. Take advantage of it if you can. Look around and keep your spirits high.

THIRTEEN

Credit-Free and Home
for the Holidays

It's the first week of December 2003, in Long Beach, California, and the real estate advertising is playing the same holiday tunes as ever: "$5,000 cash moves you in. Ready for Holidays! 3 bdrm., 2 ba., remodeled. Great financing, no qualifying! Agent xxx–xxxx."

Or how about "Belmont Shore. **RENT TO OWN** Rent Credit Available. Remodeled 3 bdrm., 2 ba. Private party: xxx–xxxx."

Downtown living for a swinging single? Try "Two East Village Studios. Under $80K. Each dwelling privately located on top floor of great building close to restaurants, shoreline, Metro, freeway, beach, and downtown commercial center. Owner May Carry. Broker: xxx–xxxx."

So what'll it be? Take your pick. And don't be shy about insisting on your terms. If one seller won't accept your no-credit arrangement, the next one might. It all depends on how badly the owners want to sell their property. That, and how well you can present your offer.

EACH ONE A GEM

"Owner walk away. Take over payments, pay closing costs, give owner $2,000 and it's yours! Open House Sunday, xxx Mountain View Dr. Agt: xxx–xxxx." The ad was fetching enough to risk a look, and author Robert Yamaguchi drove on by. The house was in a charming neighborhood of San Diego called Normal Heights. Why would anybody "walk away" from a house on that street? Perhaps the place was in terribly dilapidated condition?

Unfortunately, however, it was in fine condition. It was a cute little house with a living room designed around a bar, which had a window view of the back-yard deck and gardens. Two bedrooms, one bath, fully remodeled, two-car garage, fenced yard, great street, middle-class neighborhood, good freeway access. The price was $165,000, of which the seller owed a mort-gage balance of $161,000.

That's no profit at all for the seller. In fact, by the time he pays the agent's commission, it's a loss. So why would he walk away? Turns out the sellers had refi-nanced their loan by convincing the lender that the house was appraised at $190,000. Anyone with $2,000 and the closing costs could take over their payments while they divorced and fled to Oregon.

Here's another deal hard to imagine, but real: The ad read, "Lease option. No credit. Two bedroom, two bath condo with security parking, pool, spa, view." The owner was a sixty-year-old woman who wanted to sell the condo for retirement income, but not for four more years. So she offered it on a four-year lease with a purchase option at the end.

The way it worked was that the buyer would put down $1,600 to move in, then pay $800 a month for the first year, $100 of which applied toward the purchase. Every year, the rent went up a bit (to $835 the second year, $865 the third, and $900 the fourth) and so did the amount applied toward the buy, as it was assumed that the condo would be worth more with the passage of time. At the end of four years, buyer and seller would negotiate the price of the condo based on an appraisal, so there was no actual fixed price on the unit. A highly unusual seller's gambit.

The arrangement is odd, and potentially dangerous. What if the seller or buyer didn't agree with the appraisal after four years? Who gets to set the price? And what if the value of the condo went down in that time, always a possibility?

Anyway, Robert inspected this wonder and found it located in a complex of sixty-five apartments at the end of a cul-de-sac overlooking Fletcher Parkway, one of the smoggiest and busiest avenues of La Mesa, a suburb of San Diego. The "view" mentioned in the ad was a view of that roaring boulevard and a huge Mobil gas station that was directly below the unit's bedroom windows. The upstairs neighbor had allowed his bathtub to overflow to the extent that the roof caved in on one of the lady's two bathrooms. In general, the condo complex was rundown and possibly gang-infested. Robert wouldn't invest in it, but sure enough somebody else took that four-year lease option deal in less than a month.

Happier stories abound. The best of these tend to involve renters who manage to convince their landlords to sell them the house they already occupy. Take, for example, Don and Rosa Doner of Carmel Highlands in California, who purchased their small cottage from their longtime landlady and friend, Cynthia Williams, and spent many happy years there charming the neighbors, cooking gourmet community dinners, and entertaining the likes of scientist Linus Pauling, photographer Ansel Adams, and novelist Henry Miller as well as noncelebrities like author Ray Mungo.

If you want to convince your own landlord to sell you the house, perhaps the holiday season is as good a time as any. Some amount of sentiment may come into play, assuming you have a decent relationship as tenants to landlord. Offer him or her an installment sale, in which he gets a handsome mortgage payment every month, makes a lot more money because of the interest, and is relieved of the costs of maintaining and keeping the place up. If he or she is worried about capital gains taxes (which may be altered by ongoing federal legislation), offer an interest-only loan, free of capital gains. The principal owed never changes during the life of the loan, and the landlord only has to pay tax on the interest income. (At the end of the loan period or when the house is resold, the principal must be paid.)

Credit is a confidence game, in this respect. The seller needs to believe in YOU, in your ability to pay. Whatever it takes to inspire that belief is what you need to do, and of course the house itself is always the foundation, or collateral on the loan that the seller can fall back on if you fail. But failure is not a word in your vocabulary. In the case of no-qualifying assumable mortgages, no confidence is required. Such mortgages are simply and purely available to anyone who picks up the payments. But in seller financing and most of the other no-credit buying plans described in this book, you need help. You need someone other than a bank or lending institution or computer software application that judges you by a score you can't instantly change. You need someone to extend you a personal kind of credit. A faith. A love. A home.

If we did our job well, this book has given you a number of ideas and maybe even the inspiration to buy a home without needing to qualify for a mortgage, without needing credit. It's not only possible, but popular. Even though the conventional home purchase always requires credit, millions of people have acquired real estate without it.

Remember these main points:

• **Look for an assumable mortgage with no qualifying.** The older ones, insured by the federal government from the Federal Housing Administration (FHA) and Department of Veterans Affairs (VA) are great if you can find them, but because they originate before 1988, they are few and are generally worth far less than the current price of a house. But some nongovernment mortgages are also assumable without qualifying, at times because the seller's credit remains on the line even after he has sold the property. The previous owner's credit secures the mortgage, while you, the new owner, actually make the payments. A bank or mortgage lender has a certain amount of flexibility, and many will not call in a loan or exercise a due-on-sale clause especially if the old mortgage is at a higher interest than current rates. You can also buy the house subject to its existing mortgage, different from assuming because the mortgage remains in the seller's name although the buyer takes legal ownership and makes the payments after buying out the seller's equity. Be aggressive in this pursuit. You might be able to assume. Don't assume otherwise.

• **Buy directly from the seller, with the "owner will carry" system.** It is profitable and very easy to purchase real estate by paying the mortgage to the previous owner. All you need is a cooperative seller who either owns the house free and clear or is capable of doing a wraparound in which he continues paying his old mortgage and you pay a new one directly to him. You can offer an installment sale, an interest-only mortgage, or a short loan period (perhaps five years) capped with a balloon payment that gives you time to refinance.

• **Lease a house with an option to buy it.** That will get you a foot in the door of home ownership, and a part of every rent check you write will go toward your down payment. That also buys you some time to get your financing together, or perhaps to convince the seller to carry a first or second mortgage for you after you've established a good payment record and earned his trust.

- **Save up or otherwise acquire a 30 percent down payment.** Although it's not a rule, many banks and lenders will issue you a mortgage for the remaining 70 percent of the price of the house, even if your credit isn't good, if you come up with a big 30 percent down payment. New alternative financing waives an old prejudice against family members pooling their resources to scrape up a down payment, but it's still easier to do this if you can prove that you saved the money. This 30/70 rule flies in the face of conventional wisdom that you should never pay more than 20 percent in a down payment (because it ties up too much money), but if you lack credit, the 30 percent down payment can be the one thing that makes the deal possible.

- **Acquire title through adverse possession.** This is tricky and the laws vary from state to state, but you can take over abandoned property through open, hostile, notorious, continuous, and exclusive use, and eventually gain legal title by suing in court in a quiet title action.

- **Get into an equity-sharing partnership.** Team up with a parent, sibling, investor, or friend, and buy real estate together by sharing equity. You do the work and make the payments while someone else puts up the down payment and credit for the mortgage. Or you become a member of a group that takes title as a cooperative or corporate owner. Or you simply split the costs evenly with your partner(s) and everyone shares the living space. There are endless variations on the theme of equity sharing. It's a step up from being a renter and might improve your credit at the same time.

• **Buy a house in foreclosure, or threatened with foreclosure.** Certain foreclosure specialists will sell a home without needing credit after buying it cheap at auction. Also, homes that are about to go into foreclosure may be available without credit to anyone who will take over the payments and save the owner from losing his credit rating in a damaging foreclosure judgment.

• **Get a friend or relative to quitclaim to you.** Buy with a partner who has good credit, then have that wonderful person simply deed you his or her portion of the property by filing a quitclaim form. No method in the book is simpler than this, but of course the giver of the quitclaim remains liable for the mortgage should you default or fall behind in the payments, so you're likely to get this service only from a very close friend or family member.

• **Acquire real estate from the elderly or deceased.** Legally and ethically, of course. You can take title through a life estate, *en viager* purchase plan, reverse mortgage, or probate sale. You can negotiate a sale that gives the elderly seller a lifetime guarantee of being able to stay in the home, as well as extra income to make their retirement years secure and comfortable.

• **Look for property in trouble, or real estate that is flawed.** These unwanted, desperate, and ugly properties may be available to you without credit and may be remodeled, resuscitated, or otherwise fixed up to turn an eyesore into a pretty nice place. Also, look for sellers in trouble, people whose personal economic circumstances are forcing them to unload their property quickly. Look for trouble and you'll find it.

• **Be honest, forthright, and fearless in your quest.** Don't waste your own and others' time looking at houses that you can't afford or that require credit. Make it clear to agents and sellers that you need a no-credit transaction, and you'll find that you *can* indeed succeed!

• **Write if you like it.** Make your offer in writing. Document everything. He who writes best, and writes fastest, has the greatest chance of success. Write to us and let us know your experiences. Write and win, buy without credit, and enjoy all the tremendous advantages of owning your own home.

GLOSSARY

OF REAL ESTATE TERMS

Adverse possession. Home ownership achieved through open and unpermitted occupancy of a property over a given period of time, during which the adverse possessor pays the real estate taxes.

Amortization. A payout schedule of monthly mortgage payments, including principal and interest. The percentage of interest declines, and principal increases, with each payment.

Appraisal. An estimate of the value of a home, made by a licensed professional inspector who is a disinterested party not under any obligation to either seller or buyer.

As is. A condition set by the seller that states that he or she will not be responsible for any defects in the property.

Assessment. An official ruling of the value of a home, made by a local government agency (usually the county) for the purpose of calculating taxes on the property.

Assumable mortgage. A mortgage loan that the buyer can take over from the seller, making the same payments over the same term.

Balloon payment.   A payment due on a specific date that cashes the seller or the lender out of the entire mortgage balance owed.

Closing costs.   Expenses paid to the escrow holder for the service of processing the home-sale transaction.

Condominium, condo.   A private living unit located in a multi-unit complex, such as an apartment or townhome. Each condo is individually owned, but the complex has common areas used by all the owners, and usually a collective homeowners' association is responsible for insurance and upkeep of the complex.

Contract.   A written agreement between two parties for the sale of property.

Credit report.   A report on an individual's debts and history of making payments, compiled by a credit bureau and available to creditors and borrowers.

Deed (or Title).   A written, official declaration that transfers legal ownership of real estate and is recorded by a government agency, usually a county registrar.

Default.   The failure to make mortgage payments when due, leading to repossession of the property by the mortgage holder.

Earnest money.   A deposit paid by a buyer to a seller in evidence of good faith, which is applied to the purchase price.

Easement.   A right-of-way, or legal right to use someone else's property.

En viager.   A French system of purchasing real estate from the elderly in exchange for a down payment and monthly payments, with the elderly seller entitled to life occupancy of the home.

Equity. The amount or value that the owner holds in property, above the balance owed on the mortgage. The difference between the mortgage balance and the fair market value of the home.

Equity sharing. Shared ownership of property among two or more persons, with shares divided by mutual agreement.

Escrow. A fund and legal documents held by a trust and disbursed to seller and buyer at the successful conclusion of the sale.

FHA. Acronym for the Federal Housing Administration, an agency of the U.S. government that guarantees (insures) mortgages issued by banks and lenders.

FICO. Acronym for Fair, Isaac, & Co., a credit rating agency that issues a score rating an individual's creditworthiness, on a spectrum from 300 to 800 points. The FICO score is used by many lenders to determine qualifications for a mortgage.

Fixtures. Items in the home that are permanently attached and included in the sale of the property.

Foreclosure. The act of a lender or mortgage holder to repossess property from an owner who has failed to make payments.

Foundation. The underlying support structure of a house beneath the ground floor, such as poured concrete or a full basement.

HUD. Acronym for the U.S. Department of Housing and Urban Development. This agency sells foreclosed homes that have been insured by the federal government.

Interest. A fee paid for the loan of money, calculated as a percentage. Fixed interest rates stay the same, whereas adjustable interest rates fluctuate with the state of the economy.

Judgment. A court decision that establishes a debt owed, and specifies the amount. With a legal judgment, a creditor can attach funds or real property of a debtor to satisfy the amount owed.

Lease option. A contract between seller and prospective buyer that allows the prospective buyer to rent the home for a specific period of time and monthly rent, with the right to purchase it for a specific price at any time in the length of the agreement.

Listing. A real estate agent or broker's legal right to sell a property. An announcement of property available for purchase.

Market value. The fair price of a home, based on the amounts that comparable homes in the same vicinity have sold for in recent months.

Mortgage. A legal debt for the amount owed on a piece of property, paid by the owner to the mortgage holder, which can be an individual (the seller) or institution (bank, savings and loan, credit union, or mortgage company).

Principal. The amount of money borrowed and owed on a real estate purchase.

Probate. A court proceeding in which the property of a deceased person is distributed to heirs, after court costs are paid. If a person dies without a will (intestate), the probate court will determine who receives the property.

Qualifying. The act of being eligible for a mortgage based on sufficient credit.

Quiet title. A deed recorded without the previous owner being notified, in an adverse possession court case.

Quitclaim. Document giving part or full ownership from the property owner to another person(s). Does not affect the mortgage responsibility of the original owner.

Real estate. Land and buildings, real property.

Seller financing. A real estate sale in which the seller carries the mortgage and the buyer makes payments directly to the seller instead of to the bank or lender.

Septic tank. A private sewage disposal system buried underground near a house, when public or city-managed sewer disposal is not available.

Taxes. An annual sum, or assessment, paid to a government agency and based on the official value of the home.

30/70 rule, The. Home purchase in which the buyer puts up a down payment of at least 30 percent of the price.

Time-share. A form of ownership in which the buyer has the right to use the premises for a specific number of days per year.

Title (or Deed). Ownership of real property.

Title insurance. An insurance policy that

protects the homeowner in the event that his or her title is defective.

VA.   Acronym for the U.S. Department of Veterans Affairs.

Wraparound mortgage.   A loan in which the buyer makes mortgage payments directly to the seller, who in turn continues to make payments on his or her earlier, underlying mortgage on the same property.

INDEX